C-33 CAREER EXAMINATION SERIES

This is your
PASSBOOK for...

Assistant Civil Engineer

Test Preparation Study Guide
Questions & Answers

NATIONAL LEARNING CORPORATION®

COPYRIGHT NOTICE

This book is SOLELY intended for, is sold ONLY to, and its use is RESTRICTED to individual, bona fide applicants or candidates who qualify by virtue of having seriously filed applications for appropriate license, certificate, professional and/or promotional advancement, higher school matriculation, scholarship, or other legitimate requirements of education and/or governmental authorities.

This book is NOT intended for use, class instruction, tutoring, training, duplication, copying, reprinting, excerption, or adaptation, etc., by:

1) Other publishers
2) Proprietors and/or Instructors of "Coaching" and/or Preparatory Courses
3) Personnel and/or Training Divisions of commercial, industrial, and governmental organizations
4) Schools, colleges, or universities and/or their departments and staffs, including teachers and other personnel
5) Testing Agencies or Bureaus
6) Study groups which seek by the purchase of a single volume to copy and/or duplicate and/or adapt this material for use by the group as a whole without having purchased individual volumes for each of the members of the group
7) Et al.

Such persons would be in violation of appropriate Federal and State statutes.

PROVISION OF LICENSING AGREEMENTS – Recognized educational, commercial, industrial, and governmental institutions and organizations, and others legitimately engaged in educational pursuits, including training, testing, and measurement activities, may address request for a licensing agreement to the copyright owners, who will determine whether, and under what conditions, including fees and charges, the materials in this book may be used them. In other words, a licensing facility exists for the legitimate use of the material in this book on other than an individual basis. However, it is asseverated and affirmed here that the material in this book CANNOT be used without the receipt of the express permission of such a licensing agreement from the Publishers. Inquiries re licensing should be addressed to the company, attention rights and permissions department.

All rights reserved, including the right of reproduction in whole or in part, in any form or by any means, electronic or mechanical, including photocopying, recording, or by any information storage and retrieval system, without permission in writing from the Publisher.

Copyright © 2025 by
National Learning Corporation

212 Michael Drive, Syosset, NY 11791
(516) 921-8888 • www.passbooks.com
E-mail: info@passbooks.com

PASSBOOK® SERIES

THE *PASSBOOK® SERIES* has been created to prepare applicants and candidates for the ultimate academic battlefield – the examination room.

At some time in our lives, each and every one of us may be required to take an examination – for validation, matriculation, admission, qualification, registration, certification, or licensure.

Based on the assumption that every applicant or candidate has met the basic formal educational standards, has taken the required number of courses, and read the necessary texts, the *PASSBOOK® SERIES* furnishes the one special preparation which may assure passing with confidence, instead of failing with insecurity. Examination questions – together with answers – are furnished as the basic vehicle for study so that the mysteries of the examination and its compounding difficulties may be eliminated or diminished by a sure method.

This book is meant to help you pass your examination provided that you qualify and are serious in your objective.

The entire field is reviewed through the huge store of content information which is succinctly presented through a provocative and challenging approach – the question-and-answer method.

A climate of success is established by furnishing the correct answers at the end of each test.

You soon learn to recognize types of questions, forms of questions, and patterns of questioning. You may even begin to anticipate expected outcomes.

You perceive that many questions are repeated or adapted so that you can gain acute insights, which may enable you to score many sure points.

You learn how to confront new questions, or types of questions, and to attack them confidently and work out the correct answers.

You note objectives and emphases, and recognize pitfalls and dangers, so that you may make positive educational adjustments.

Moreover, you are kept fully informed in relation to new concepts, methods, practices, and directions in the field.

You discover that you are actually taking the examination all the time: you are preparing for the examination by "taking" an examination, not by reading extraneous and/or supererogatory textbooks.

In short, this PASSBOOK®, used directedly, should be an important factor in helping you to pass your test.

ASSISTANT CIVIL ENGINEER

DUTIES
Under supervision, performs civil engineering work of moderate difficulty and responsibility; may supervise subordinate employees.

An employee in this class receives assignments requiring the application of engineering skills and knowledges to civil engineering projects in connection with the design, construction, inspection, operation and maintenance of public works, including the planning and monitoring of sewage treatment systems and facilities. Assignments are received with general instructions, but incumbents are expected to use initiative and judgment in completing them. Supervision may be exercised over technical assistants in any phase of their assigned duties. Work is reviewed while in progress and upon conclusion by a technical supervisor for the achievement of desired results.

EXAMPLES OF TYPICAL TASKS
Supervises a small squad, unit or group engaged in the performance of work in design, construction, supervision, inspection and testing, or drafting and tracing. Engages in research, investigation, studies or examinations related to the engineering functions or activities of a department or agency. Develops drawings. Writes specifications and prepares estimates of quantities. Participates in field surveys as chief of party or in other capacities. Participates in inspection operations by observing, checking and certifying the installation of materials and equipment. Attests to equipment performance and tests of materials. Reviews or examines plans for the construction, demolition or alteration of structures to comply with the provisions of law, rule or regulation.

SCOPE OF THE EXAMINATION
The multiple-choice test may include questions on civil engineering design principles and theories; construction techniques, methodology, materials and equipment; surveying; drafting; mathematics; preparation of contract drawings and specifications; safe working practices; principles of supervision; and other related areas.

HOW TO TAKE A TEST

I. YOU MUST PASS AN EXAMINATION

A. WHAT EVERY CANDIDATE SHOULD KNOW

Examination applicants often ask us for help in preparing for the written test. What can I study in advance? What kinds of questions will be asked? How will the test be given? How will the papers be graded?

As an applicant for a civil service examination, you may be wondering about some of these things. Our purpose here is to suggest effective methods of advance study and to describe civil service examinations.

Your chances for success on this examination can be increased if you know how to prepare. Those "pre-examination jitters" can be reduced if you know what to expect. You can even experience an adventure in good citizenship if you know why civil service exams are given.

B. WHY ARE CIVIL SERVICE EXAMINATIONS GIVEN?

Civil service examinations are important to you in two ways. As a citizen, you want public jobs filled by employees who know how to do their work. As a job seeker, you want a fair chance to compete for that job on an equal footing with other candidates. The best-known means of accomplishing this two-fold goal is the competitive examination.

Exams are widely publicized throughout the nation. They may be administered for jobs in federal, state, city, municipal, town or village governments or agencies.

Any citizen may apply, with some limitations, such as the age or residence of applicants. Your experience and education may be reviewed to see whether you meet the requirements for the particular examination. When these requirements exist, they are reasonable and applied consistently to all applicants. Thus, a competitive examination may cause you some uneasiness now, but it is your privilege and safeguard.

C. HOW ARE CIVIL SERVICE EXAMS DEVELOPED?

Examinations are carefully written by trained technicians who are specialists in the field known as "psychological measurement," in consultation with recognized authorities in the field of work that the test will cover. These experts recommend the subject matter areas or skills to be tested; only those knowledges or skills important to your success on the job are included. The most reliable books and source materials available are used as references. Together, the experts and technicians judge the difficulty level of the questions.

Test technicians know how to phrase questions so that the problem is clearly stated. Their ethics do not permit "trick" or "catch" questions. Questions may have been tried out on sample groups, or subjected to statistical analysis, to determine their usefulness.

Written tests are often used in combination with performance tests, ratings of training and experience, and oral interviews. All of these measures combine to form the best-known means of finding the right person for the right job.

II. HOW TO PASS THE WRITTEN TEST

A. NATURE OF THE EXAMINATION

To prepare intelligently for civil service examinations, you should know how they differ from school examinations you have taken. In school you were assigned certain definite pages to read or subjects to cover. The examination questions were quite detailed and usually emphasized memory. Civil service exams, on the other hand, try to discover your present ability to perform the duties of a position, plus your potentiality to learn these duties. In other words, a civil service exam attempts to predict how successful you will be. Questions cover such a broad area that they cannot be as minute and detailed as school exam questions.

In the public service similar kinds of work, or positions, are grouped together in one "class." This process is known as *position-classification*. All the positions in a class are paid according to the salary range for that class. One class title covers all of these positions, and they are all tested by the same examination.

B. FOUR BASIC STEPS

1) Study the announcement

How, then, can you know what subjects to study? Our best answer is: "Learn as much as possible about the class of positions for which you've applied." The exam will test the knowledge, skills and abilities needed to do the work.

Your most valuable source of information about the position you want is the official exam announcement. This announcement lists the training and experience qualifications. Check these standards and apply only if you come reasonably close to meeting them.

The brief description of the position in the examination announcement offers some clues to the subjects which will be tested. Think about the job itself. Review the duties in your mind. Can you perform them, or are there some in which you are rusty? Fill in the blank spots in your preparation.

Many jurisdictions preview the written test in the exam announcement by including a section called "Knowledge and Abilities Required," "Scope of the Examination," or some similar heading. Here you will find out specifically what fields will be tested.

2) Review your own background

Once you learn in general what the position is all about, and what you need to know to do the work, ask yourself which subjects you already know fairly well and which need improvement. You may wonder whether to concentrate on improving your strong areas or on building some background in your fields of weakness. When the announcement has specified "some knowledge" or "considerable knowledge," or has used adjectives like "beginning principles of…" or "advanced … methods," you can get a clue as to the number and difficulty of questions to be asked in any given field. More questions, and hence broader coverage, would be included for those subjects which are more important in the work. Now weigh your strengths and weaknesses against the job requirements and prepare accordingly.

3) Determine the level of the position

Another way to tell how intensively you should prepare is to understand the level of the job for which you are applying. Is it the entering level? In other words, is this the position in which beginners in a field of work are hired? Or is it an intermediate or advanced level? Sometimes this is indicated by such words as "Junior" or "Senior" in the class title. Other jurisdictions use Roman numerals to designate the level – Clerk I, Clerk II, for example. The word "Supervisor" sometimes appears in the title. If the level is not indicated by the title, check the description of duties. Will you be working under very close supervision, or will you have responsibility for independent decisions in this work?

4) Choose appropriate study materials

Now that you know the subjects to be examined and the relative amount of each subject to be covered, you can choose suitable study materials. For beginning level jobs, or even advanced ones, if you have a pronounced weakness in some aspect of your training, read a modern, standard textbook in that field. Be sure it is up to date and has general coverage. Such books are normally available at your library, and the librarian will be glad to help you locate one. For entry-level positions, questions of appropriate difficulty are chosen – neither highly advanced questions, nor those too simple. Such questions require careful thought but not advanced training.

If the position for which you are applying is technical or advanced, you will read more advanced, specialized material. If you are already familiar with the basic principles of your field, elementary textbooks would waste your time. Concentrate on advanced textbooks and technical periodicals. Think through the concepts and review difficult problems in your field.

These are all general sources. You can get more ideas on your own initiative, following these leads. For example, training manuals and publications of the government agency which employs workers in your field can be useful, particularly for technical and professional positions. A letter or visit to the government department involved may result in more specific study suggestions, and certainly will provide you with a more definite idea of the exact nature of the position you are seeking.

III. KINDS OF TESTS

Tests are used for purposes other than measuring knowledge and ability to perform specified duties. For some positions, it is equally important to test ability to make adjustments to new situations or to profit from training. In others, basic mental abilities not dependent on information are essential. Questions which test these things may not appear as pertinent to the duties of the position as those which test for knowledge and information. Yet they are often highly important parts of a fair examination. For very general questions, it is almost impossible to help you direct your study efforts. What we can do is to point out some of the more common of these general abilities needed in public service positions and describe some typical questions.

1) General information

Broad, general information has been found useful for predicting job success in some kinds of work. This is tested in a variety of ways, from vocabulary lists to questions about current events. Basic background in some field of work, such as sociology or economics, may be sampled in a group of questions. Often these are principles which have become familiar to most persons through exposure rather than through formal training. It is difficult to advise you how to study for these questions; being alert to the world around you is our best suggestion.

2) Verbal ability

An example of an ability needed in many positions is verbal or language ability. Verbal ability is, in brief, the ability to use and understand words. Vocabulary and grammar tests are typical measures of this ability. Reading comprehension or paragraph interpretation questions are common in many kinds of civil service tests. You are given a paragraph of written material and asked to find its central meaning.

3) Numerical ability

Number skills can be tested by the familiar arithmetic problem, by checking paired lists of numbers to see which are alike and which are different, or by interpreting charts and graphs. In the latter test, a graph may be printed in the test booklet which you are asked to use as the basis for answering questions.

4) Observation

A popular test for law-enforcement positions is the observation test. A picture is shown to you for several minutes, then taken away. Questions about the picture test your ability to observe both details and larger elements.

5) Following directions

In many positions in the public service, the employee must be able to carry out written instructions dependably and accurately. You may be given a chart with several columns, each column listing a variety of information. The questions require you to carry out directions involving the information given in the chart.

6) Skills and aptitudes

Performance tests effectively measure some manual skills and aptitudes. When the skill is one in which you are trained, such as typing or shorthand, you can practice. These tests are often very much like those given in business school or high school courses. For many of the other skills and aptitudes, however, no short-time preparation can be made. Skills and abilities natural to you or that you have developed throughout your lifetime are being tested.

Many of the general questions just described provide all the data needed to answer the questions and ask you to use your reasoning ability to find the answers. Your best preparation for these tests, as well as for tests of facts and ideas, is to be at your physical and mental best. You, no doubt, have your own methods of getting into an exam-taking mood and keeping "in shape." The next section lists some ideas on this subject.

IV. KINDS OF QUESTIONS

Only rarely is the "essay" question, which you answer in narrative form, used in civil service tests. Civil service tests are usually of the short-answer type. Full instructions for answering these questions will be given to you at the examination. But in case this is your first experience with short-answer questions and separate answer sheets, here is what you need to know:

1) Multiple-choice Questions

Most popular of the short-answer questions is the "multiple choice" or "best answer" question. It can be used, for example, to test for factual knowledge, ability to solve problems or judgment in meeting situations found at work.

A multiple-choice question is normally one of three types—
- It can begin with an incomplete statement followed by several possible endings. You are to find the one ending which *best* completes the statement, although some of the others may not be entirely wrong.
- It can also be a complete statement in the form of a question which is answered by choosing one of the statements listed.

- It can be in the form of a problem – again you select the best answer.

Here is an example of a multiple-choice question with a discussion which should give you some clues as to the method for choosing the right answer:

When an employee has a complaint about his assignment, the action which will *best* help him overcome his difficulty is to
  A. discuss his difficulty with his coworkers
  B. take the problem to the head of the organization
  C. take the problem to the person who gave him the assignment
  D. say nothing to anyone about his complaint

In answering this question, you should study each of the choices to find which is best. Consider choice "A" – Certainly an employee may discuss his complaint with fellow employees, but no change or improvement can result, and the complaint remains unresolved. Choice "B" is a poor choice since the head of the organization probably does not know what assignment you have been given, and taking your problem to him is known as "going over the head" of the supervisor. The supervisor, or person who made the assignment, is the person who can clarify it or correct any injustice. Choice "C" is, therefore, correct. To say nothing, as in choice "D," is unwise. Supervisors have and interest in knowing the problems employees are facing, and the employee is seeking a solution to his problem.

2) True/False Questions

The "true/false" or "right/wrong" form of question is sometimes used. Here a complete statement is given. Your job is to decide whether the statement is right or wrong.

SAMPLE: A roaming cell-phone call to a nearby city costs less than a non-roaming call to a distant city.

This statement is wrong, or false, since roaming calls are more expensive.

This is not a complete list of all possible question forms, although most of the others are variations of these common types. You will always get complete directions for answering questions. Be sure you understand *how* to mark your answers – ask questions until you do.

V. RECORDING YOUR ANSWERS

Computer terminals are used more and more today for many different kinds of exams.
For an examination with very few applicants, you may be told to record your answers in the test booklet itself. Separate answer sheets are much more common. If this separate answer sheet is to be scored by machine – and this is often the case – it is highly important that you mark your answers correctly in order to get credit.
An electronic scoring machine is often used in civil service offices because of the speed with which papers can be scored. Machine-scored answer sheets must be marked with a pencil, which will be given to you. This pencil has a high graphite content which responds to the electronic scoring machine. As a matter of fact, stray dots may register as answers, so do not let your pencil rest on the answer sheet while you are pondering the correct answer. Also, if your pencil lead breaks or is otherwise defective, ask for another.

Since the answer sheet will be dropped in a slot in the scoring machine, be careful not to bend the corners or get the paper crumpled.

The answer sheet normally has five vertical columns of numbers, with 30 numbers to a column. These numbers correspond to the question numbers in your test booklet. After each number, going across the page are four or five pairs of dotted lines. These short dotted lines have small letters or numbers above them. The first two pairs may also have a "T" or "F" above the letters. This indicates that the first two pairs only are to be used if the questions are of the true-false type. If the questions are multiple choice, disregard the "T" and "F" and pay attention only to the small letters or numbers.

Answer your questions in the manner of the sample that follows:

32. The largest city in the United States is
    A. Washington, D.C.
    B. New York City
    C. Chicago
    D. Detroit
    E. San Francisco

1) Choose the answer you think is best. (New York City is the largest, so "B" is correct.)
2) Find the row of dotted lines numbered the same as the question you are answering. (Find row number 32)
3) Find the pair of dotted lines corresponding to the answer. (Find the pair of lines under the mark "B.")
4) Make a solid black mark between the dotted lines.

VI. BEFORE THE TEST

Common sense will help you find procedures to follow to get ready for an examination. Too many of us, however, overlook these sensible measures. Indeed, nervousness and fatigue have been found to be the most serious reasons why applicants fail to do their best on civil service tests. Here is a list of reminders:

- Begin your preparation early – Don't wait until the last minute to go scurrying around for books and materials or to find out what the position is all about.
- Prepare continuously – An hour a night for a week is better than an all-night cram session. This has been definitely established. What is more, a night a week for a month will return better dividends than crowding your study into a shorter period of time.
- Locate the place of the exam – You have been sent a notice telling you when and where to report for the examination. If the location is in a different town or otherwise unfamiliar to you, it would be well to inquire the best route and learn something about the building.
- Relax the night before the test – Allow your mind to rest. Do not study at all that night. Plan some mild recreation or diversion; then go to bed early and get a good night's sleep.
- Get up early enough to make a leisurely trip to the place for the test – This way unforeseen events, traffic snarls, unfamiliar buildings, etc. will not upset you.
- Dress comfortably – A written test is not a fashion show. You will be known by number and not by name, so wear something comfortable.

- Leave excess paraphernalia at home – Shopping bags and odd bundles will get in your way. You need bring only the items mentioned in the official notice you received; usually everything you need is provided. Do not bring reference books to the exam. They will only confuse those last minutes and be taken away from you when in the test room.
- Arrive somewhat ahead of time – If because of transportation schedules you must get there very early, bring a newspaper or magazine to take your mind off yourself while waiting.
- Locate the examination room – When you have found the proper room, you will be directed to the seat or part of the room where you will sit. Sometimes you are given a sheet of instructions to read while you are waiting. Do not fill out any forms until you are told to do so; just read them and be prepared.
- Relax and prepare to listen to the instructions
- If you have any physical problem that may keep you from doing your best, be sure to tell the test administrator. If you are sick or in poor health, you really cannot do your best on the exam. You can come back and take the test some other time.

VII. AT THE TEST

The day of the test is here and you have the test booklet in your hand. The temptation to get going is very strong. Caution! There is more to success than knowing the right answers. You must know how to identify your papers and understand variations in the type of short-answer question used in this particular examination. Follow these suggestions for maximum results from your efforts:

1) Cooperate with the monitor

The test administrator has a duty to create a situation in which you can be as much at ease as possible. He will give instructions, tell you when to begin, check to see that you are marking your answer sheet correctly, and so on. He is not there to guard you, although he will see that your competitors do not take unfair advantage. He wants to help you do your best.

2) Listen to all instructions

Don't jump the gun! Wait until you understand all directions. In most civil service tests you get more time than you need to answer the questions. So don't be in a hurry. Read each word of instructions until you clearly understand the meaning. Study the examples, listen to all announcements and follow directions. Ask questions if you do not understand what to do.

3) Identify your papers

Civil service exams are usually identified by number only. You will be assigned a number; you must not put your name on your test papers. Be sure to copy your number correctly. Since more than one exam may be given, copy your exact examination title.

4) Plan your time

Unless you are told that a test is a "speed" or "rate of work" test, speed itself is usually not important. Time enough to answer all the questions will be provided, but this does not mean that you have all day. An overall time limit has been set. Divide the total time (in minutes) by the number of questions to determine the approximate time you have for each question.

5) Do not linger over difficult questions

If you come across a difficult question, mark it with a paper clip (useful to have along) and come back to it when you have been through the booklet. One caution if you do this – be sure to skip a number on your answer sheet as well. Check often to be sure that you have not lost your place and that you are marking in the row numbered the same as the question you are answering.

6) Read the questions

Be sure you know what the question asks! Many capable people are unsuccessful because they failed to *read* the questions correctly.

7) Answer all questions

Unless you have been instructed that a penalty will be deducted for incorrect answers, it is better to guess than to omit a question.

8) Speed tests

It is often better NOT to guess on speed tests. It has been found that on timed tests people are tempted to spend the last few seconds before time is called in marking answers at random – without even reading them – in the hope of picking up a few extra points. To discourage this practice, the instructions may warn you that your score will be "corrected" for guessing. That is, a penalty will be applied. The incorrect answers will be deducted from the correct ones, or some other penalty formula will be used.

9) Review your answers

If you finish before time is called, go back to the questions you guessed or omitted to give them further thought. Review other answers if you have time.

10) Return your test materials

If you are ready to leave before others have finished or time is called, take ALL your materials to the monitor and leave quietly. Never take any test material with you. The monitor can discover whose papers are not complete, and taking a test booklet may be grounds for disqualification.

VIII. EXAMINATION TECHNIQUES

1) Read the general instructions carefully. These are usually printed on the first page of the exam booklet. As a rule, these instructions refer to the timing of the examination; the fact that you should not start work until the signal and must stop work at a signal, etc. If there are any *special* instructions, such as a choice of questions to be answered, make sure that you note this instruction carefully.

2) When you are ready to start work on the examination, that is as soon as the signal has been given, read the instructions to each question booklet, underline any key words or phrases, such as *least, best, outline, describe* and the like. In this way you will tend to answer as requested rather than discover on reviewing your paper that you *listed without describing*, that you selected the *worst* choice rather than the *best* choice, etc.

3) If the examination is of the objective or multiple-choice type – that is, each question will also give a series of possible answers: A, B, C or D, and you are called upon to select the best answer and write the letter next to that answer on your answer paper – it is advisable to start answering each question in turn. There may be anywhere from 50 to 100 such questions in the three or four hours allotted and you can see how much time would be taken if you read through all the questions before beginning to answer any. Furthermore, if you come across a question or group of questions which you know would be difficult to answer, it would undoubtedly affect your handling of all the other questions.

4) If the examination is of the essay type and contains but a few questions, it is a moot point as to whether you should read all the questions before starting to answer any one. Of course, if you are given a choice – say five out of seven and the like – then it is essential to read all the questions so you can eliminate the two that are most difficult. If, however, you are asked to answer all the questions, there may be danger in trying to answer the easiest one first because you may find that you will spend too much time on it. The best technique is to answer the first question, then proceed to the second, etc.

5) Time your answers. Before the exam begins, write down the time it started, then add the time allowed for the examination and write down the time it must be completed, then divide the time available somewhat as follows:
   - If 3-1/2 hours are allowed, that would be 210 minutes. If you have 80 objective-type questions, that would be an average of 2-1/2 minutes per question. Allow yourself no more than 2 minutes per question, or a total of 160 minutes, which will permit about 50 minutes to review.
   - If for the time allotment of 210 minutes there are 7 essay questions to answer, that would average about 30 minutes a question. Give yourself only 25 minutes per question so that you have about 35 minutes to review.

6) The most important instruction is to *read each question* and make sure you know what is wanted. The second most important instruction is to *time yourself properly* so that you answer every question. The third most important instruction is to *answer every question*. Guess if you have to but include something for each question. Remember that you will receive no credit for a blank and will probably receive some credit if you write something in answer to an essay question. If you guess a letter – say "B" for a multiple-choice question – you may have guessed right. If you leave a blank as an answer to a multiple-choice question, the examiners may respect your feelings but it will not add a point to your score. Some exams may penalize you for wrong answers, so in such cases *only*, you may not want to guess unless you have some basis for your answer.

7) Suggestions
   a. Objective-type questions
      1. Examine the question booklet for proper sequence of pages and questions
      2. Read all instructions carefully
      3. Skip any question which seems too difficult; return to it after all other questions have been answered
      4. Apportion your time properly; do not spend too much time on any single question or group of questions

5. Note and underline key words – *all, most, fewest, least, best, worst, same, opposite,* etc.
6. Pay particular attention to negatives
7. Note unusual option, e.g., unduly long, short, complex, different or similar in content to the body of the question
8. Observe the use of "hedging" words – *probably, may, most likely,* etc.
9. Make sure that your answer is put next to the same number as the question
10. Do not second-guess unless you have good reason to believe the second answer is definitely more correct
11. Cross out original answer if you decide another answer is more accurate; do not erase until you are ready to hand your paper in
12. Answer all questions; guess unless instructed otherwise
13. Leave time for review

b. Essay questions
1. Read each question carefully
2. Determine exactly what is wanted. Underline key words or phrases.
3. Decide on outline or paragraph answer
4. Include many different points and elements unless asked to develop any one or two points or elements
5. Show impartiality by giving pros and cons unless directed to select one side only
6. Make and write down any assumptions you find necessary to answer the questions
7. Watch your English, grammar, punctuation and choice of words
8. Time your answers; don't crowd material

8) Answering the essay question

Most essay questions can be answered by framing the specific response around several key words or ideas. Here are a few such key words or ideas:

M's: manpower, materials, methods, money, management
P's: purpose, program, policy, plan, procedure, practice, problems, pitfalls, personnel, public relations

a. Six basic steps in handling problems:
1. Preliminary plan and background development
2. Collect information, data and facts
3. Analyze and interpret information, data and facts
4. Analyze and develop solutions as well as make recommendations
5. Prepare report and sell recommendations
6. Install recommendations and follow up effectiveness

b. Pitfalls to avoid
1. *Taking things for granted* – A statement of the situation does not necessarily imply that each of the elements is necessarily true; for example, a complaint may be invalid and biased so that all that can be taken for granted is that a complaint has been registered

2. *Considering only one side of a situation* – Wherever possible, indicate several alternatives and then point out the reasons you selected the best one
3. *Failing to indicate follow up* – Whenever your answer indicates action on your part, make certain that you will take proper follow-up action to see how successful your recommendations, procedures or actions turn out to be
4. *Taking too long in answering any single question* – Remember to time your answers properly

IX. AFTER THE TEST

Scoring procedures differ in detail among civil service jurisdictions although the general principles are the same. Whether the papers are hand-scored or graded by machine we have described, they are nearly always graded by number. That is, the person who marks the paper knows only the number – never the name – of the applicant. Not until all the papers have been graded will they be matched with names. If other tests, such as training and experience or oral interview ratings have been given, scores will be combined. Different parts of the examination usually have different weights. For example, the written test might count 60 percent of the final grade, and a rating of training and experience 40 percent. In many jurisdictions, veterans will have a certain number of points added to their grades.

After the final grade has been determined, the names are placed in grade order and an eligible list is established. There are various methods for resolving ties between those who get the same final grade – probably the most common is to place first the name of the person whose application was received first. Job offers are made from the eligible list in the order the names appear on it. You will be notified of your grade and your rank as soon as all these computations have been made. This will be done as rapidly as possible.

People who are found to meet the requirements in the announcement are called "eligibles." Their names are put on a list of eligible candidates. An eligible's chances of getting a job depend on how high he stands on this list and how fast agencies are filling jobs from the list.

When a job is to be filled from a list of eligibles, the agency asks for the names of people on the list of eligibles for that job. When the civil service commission receives this request, it sends to the agency the names of the three people highest on this list. Or, if the job to be filled has specialized requirements, the office sends the agency the names of the top three persons who meet these requirements from the general list.

The appointing officer makes a choice from among the three people whose names were sent to him. If the selected person accepts the appointment, the names of the others are put back on the list to be considered for future openings.

That is the rule in hiring from all kinds of eligible lists, whether they are for typist, carpenter, chemist, or something else. For every vacancy, the appointing officer has his choice of any one of the top three eligibles on the list. This explains why the person whose name is on top of the list sometimes does not get an appointment when some of the persons lower on the list do. If the appointing officer chooses the second or third eligible, the No. 1 eligible does not get a job at once, but stays on the list until he is appointed or the list is terminated.

X. HOW TO PASS THE INTERVIEW TEST

The examination for which you applied requires an oral interview test. You have already taken the written test and you are now being called for the interview test – the final part of the formal examination.

You may think that it is not possible to prepare for an interview test and that there are no procedures to follow during an interview. Our purpose is to point out some things you can do in advance that will help you and some good rules to follow and pitfalls to avoid while you are being interviewed.

What is an interview supposed to test?

The written examination is designed to test the technical knowledge and competence of the candidate; the oral is designed to evaluate intangible qualities, not readily measured otherwise, and to establish a list showing the relative fitness of each candidate – as measured against his competitors – for the position sought. Scoring is not on the basis of "right" and "wrong," but on a sliding scale of values ranging from "not passable" to "outstanding." As a matter of fact, it is possible to achieve a relatively low score without a single "incorrect" answer because of evident weakness in the qualities being measured.

Occasionally, an examination may consist entirely of an oral test – either an individual or a group oral. In such cases, information is sought concerning the technical knowledges and abilities of the candidate, since there has been no written examination for this purpose. More commonly, however, an oral test is used to supplement a written examination.

Who conducts interviews?

The composition of oral boards varies among different jurisdictions. In nearly all, a representative of the personnel department serves as chairman. One of the members of the board may be a representative of the department in which the candidate would work. In some cases, "outside experts" are used, and, frequently, a businessman or some other representative of the general public is asked to serve. Labor and management or other special groups may be represented. The aim is to secure the services of experts in the appropriate field.

However the board is composed, it is a good idea (and not at all improper or unethical) to ascertain in advance of the interview who the members are and what groups they represent. When you are introduced to them, you will have some idea of their backgrounds and interests, and at least you will not stutter and stammer over their names.

What should be done before the interview?

While knowledge about the board members is useful and takes some of the surprise element out of the interview, there is other preparation which is more substantive. It *is* possible to prepare for an oral interview – in several ways:

1) Keep a copy of your application and review it carefully before the interview

This may be the only document before the oral board, and the starting point of the interview. Know what education and experience you have listed there, and the sequence and dates of all of it. Sometimes the board will ask you to review the highlights of your experience for them; you should not have to hem and haw doing it.

2) Study the class specification and the examination announcement

Usually, the oral board has one or both of these to guide them. The qualities, characteristics or knowledges required by the position sought are stated in these documents. They offer valuable clues as to the nature of the oral interview. For example, if the job involves supervisory responsibilities, the announcement will usually indicate that knowledge of modern supervisory methods and the qualifications of the candidate as a supervisor will be tested. If so, you can expect such questions, frequently in the form of a hypothetical situation which you are expected to solve. NEVER go into an oral without knowledge of the duties and responsibilities of the job you seek.

3) Think through each qualification required

Try to visualize the kind of questions you would ask if you were a board member. How well could you answer them? Try especially to appraise your own knowledge and background in each area, *measured against the job sought*, and identify any areas in which you are weak. Be critical and realistic – do not flatter yourself.

4) Do some general reading in areas in which you feel you may be weak

For example, if the job involves supervision and your past experience has NOT, some general reading in supervisory methods and practices, particularly in the field of human relations, might be useful. Do NOT study agency procedures or detailed manuals. The oral board will be testing your understanding and capacity, not your memory.

5) Get a good night's sleep and watch your general health and mental attitude

You will want a clear head at the interview. Take care of a cold or any other minor ailment, and of course, no hangovers.

What should be done on the day of the interview?

Now comes the day of the interview itself. Give yourself plenty of time to get there. Plan to arrive somewhat ahead of the scheduled time, particularly if your appointment is in the fore part of the day. If a previous candidate fails to appear, the board might be ready for you a bit early. By early afternoon an oral board is almost invariably behind schedule if there are many candidates, and you may have to wait. Take along a book or magazine to read, or your application to review, but leave any extraneous material in the waiting room when you go in for your interview. In any event, relax and compose yourself.

The matter of dress is important. The board is forming impressions about you – from your experience, your manners, your attitude, and your appearance. Give your personal appearance careful attention. Dress your best, but not your flashiest. Choose conservative, appropriate clothing, and be sure it is immaculate. This is a business interview, and your appearance should indicate that you regard it as such. Besides, being well groomed and properly dressed will help boost your confidence.

Sooner or later, someone will call your name and escort you into the interview room. *This is it.* From here on you are on your own. It is too late for any more preparation. But remember, you asked for this opportunity to prove your fitness, and you are here because your request was granted.

What happens when you go in?

The usual sequence of events will be as follows: The clerk (who is often the board stenographer) will introduce you to the chairman of the oral board, who will introduce you to the other members of the board. Acknowledge the introductions before you sit down. Do not be surprised if you find a microphone facing you or a stenotypist sitting by. Oral interviews are usually recorded in the event of an appeal or other review.

Usually the chairman of the board will open the interview by reviewing the highlights of your education and work experience from your application – primarily for the benefit of the other members of the board, as well as to get the material into the record. Do not interrupt or comment unless there is an error or significant misinterpretation; if that is the case, do not hesitate. But do not quibble about insignificant matters. Also, he will usually ask you some question about your education, experience or your present job – partly to get you to start talking and to establish the interviewing "rapport." He may start the actual questioning, or turn it over to one of the other members. Frequently, each member undertakes the questioning on a particular area, one in which he is perhaps most competent, so you can expect each member to participate in the examination. Because time is limited, you may also expect some rather abrupt switches in the direction the questioning takes, so do not be upset by it. Normally, a board member will not pursue a single line of questioning unless he discovers a particular strength or weakness.

After each member has participated, the chairman will usually ask whether any member has any further questions, then will ask you if you have anything you wish to add. Unless you are expecting this question, it may floor you. Worse, it may start you off on an extended, extemporaneous speech. The board is not usually seeking more information. The question is principally to offer you a last opportunity to present further qualifications or to indicate that you have nothing to add. So, if you feel that a significant qualification or characteristic has been overlooked, it is proper to point it out in a sentence or so. Do not compliment the board on the thoroughness of their examination – they have been sketchy, and you know it. If you wish, merely say, "No thank you, I have nothing further to add." This is a point where you can "talk yourself out" of a good impression or fail to present an important bit of information. Remember, *you close the interview yourself.*

The chairman will then say, "That is all, Mr. _____, thank you." Do not be startled; the interview is over, and quicker than you think. Thank him, gather your belongings and take your leave. Save your sigh of relief for the other side of the door.

How to put your best foot forward

Throughout this entire process, you may feel that the board individually and collectively is trying to pierce your defenses, seek out your hidden weaknesses and embarrass and confuse you. Actually, this is not true. They are obliged to make an appraisal of your qualifications for the job you are seeking, and they want to see you in your best light. Remember, they must interview all candidates and a non-cooperative candidate may become a failure in spite of their best efforts to bring out his qualifications. Here are 15 suggestions that will help you:

1) Be natural – Keep your attitude confident, not cocky

If you are not confident that you can do the job, do not expect the board to be. Do not apologize for your weaknesses, try to bring out your strong points. The board is interested in a positive, not negative, presentation. Cockiness will antagonize any board member and make him wonder if you are covering up a weakness by a false show of strength.

2) Get comfortable, but don't lounge or sprawl

Sit erectly but not stiffly. A careless posture may lead the board to conclude that you are careless in other things, or at least that you are not impressed by the importance of the occasion. Either conclusion is natural, even if incorrect. Do not fuss with your clothing, a pencil or an ashtray. Your hands may occasionally be useful to emphasize a point; do not let them become a point of distraction.

3) Do not wisecrack or make small talk

This is a serious situation, and your attitude should show that you consider it as such. Further, the time of the board is limited – they do not want to waste it, and neither should you.

4) Do not exaggerate your experience or abilities

In the first place, from information in the application or other interviews and sources, the board may know more about you than you think. Secondly, you probably will not get away with it. An experienced board is rather adept at spotting such a situation, so do not take the chance.

5) If you know a board member, do not make a point of it, yet do not hide it

Certainly you are not fooling him, and probably not the other members of the board. Do not try to take advantage of your acquaintanceship – it will probably do you little good.

6) Do not dominate the interview

Let the board do that. They will give you the clues – do not assume that you have to do all the talking. Realize that the board has a number of questions to ask you, and do not try to take up all the interview time by showing off your extensive knowledge of the answer to the first one.

7) Be attentive

You only have 20 minutes or so, and you should keep your attention at its sharpest throughout. When a member is addressing a problem or question to you, give him your undivided attention. Address your reply principally to him, but do not exclude the other board members.

8) Do not interrupt

A board member may be stating a problem for you to analyze. He will ask you a question when the time comes. Let him state the problem, and wait for the question.

9) Make sure you understand the question

Do not try to answer until you are sure what the question is. If it is not clear, restate it in your own words or ask the board member to clarify it for you. However, do not haggle about minor elements.

10) Reply promptly but not hastily

A common entry on oral board rating sheets is "candidate responded readily," or "candidate hesitated in replies." Respond as promptly and quickly as you can, but do not jump to a hasty, ill-considered answer.

11) Do not be peremptory in your answers

A brief answer is proper – but do not fire your answer back. That is a losing game from your point of view. The board member can probably ask questions much faster than you can answer them.

12) Do not try to create the answer you think the board member wants

He is interested in what kind of mind you have and how it works – not in playing games. Furthermore, he can usually spot this practice and will actually grade you down on it.

13) Do not switch sides in your reply merely to agree with a board member

Frequently, a member will take a contrary position merely to draw you out and to see if you are willing and able to defend your point of view. Do not start a debate, yet do not surrender a good position. If a position is worth taking, it is worth defending.

14) Do not be afraid to admit an error in judgment if you are shown to be wrong

The board knows that you are forced to reply without any opportunity for careful consideration. Your answer may be demonstrably wrong. If so, admit it and get on with the interview.

15) Do not dwell at length on your present job

The opening question may relate to your present assignment. Answer the question but do not go into an extended discussion. You are being examined for a *new* job, not your present one. As a matter of fact, try to phrase ALL your answers in terms of the job for which you are being examined.

Basis of Rating

Probably you will forget most of these "do's" and "don'ts" when you walk into the oral interview room. Even remembering them all will not ensure you a passing grade. Perhaps you did not have the qualifications in the first place. But remembering them will help you to put your best foot forward, without treading on the toes of the board members.

Rumor and popular opinion to the contrary notwithstanding, an oral board wants you to make the best appearance possible. They know you are under pressure – but they also want to see how you respond to it as a guide to what your reaction would be under the pressures of the job you seek. They will be influenced by the degree of poise you display, the personal traits you show and the manner in which you respond.

ABOUT THIS BOOK

This book contains tests divided into Examination Sections. Go through each test, answering every question in the margin. We have also attached a sample answer sheet at the back of the book that can be removed and used. At the end of each test look at the answer key and check your answers. On the ones you got wrong, look at the right answer choice and learn. Do not fill in the answers first. Do not memorize the questions and answers, but understand the answer and principles involved. On your test, the questions will likely be different from the samples. Questions are changed and new ones added. If you understand these past questions you should have success with any changes that arise. Tests may consist of several types of questions. We have additional books on each subject should more study be advisable or necessary for you. Finally, the more you study, the better prepared you will be. This book is intended to be the last thing you study before you walk into the examination room. Prior study of relevant texts is also recommended. NLC publishes some of these in our Fundamental Series. Knowledge and good sense are important factors in passing your exam. Good luck also helps. So now study this Passbook, absorb the material contained within and take that knowledge into the examination. Then do your best to pass that exam.

EXAMINATION SECTION

EXAMINATION SECTION
TEST 1

DIRECTIONS: Each question or incomplete statement is followed by several suggested answers or completions. Select the one that BEST answers the question or completes the Statement. *PRINT THE LETTER OF THE CORRECT ANSWER IN THE SPACE AT THE RIGHT.*

1. The P.C. of a 7-degree curve is at Sta 16 + 25.0. The deflection angle to Sta 17 + 00 is *most clearly*

   A. 5°15'   B. 3°30'   C. 2°38'   D. 1°45'

   1._____

2.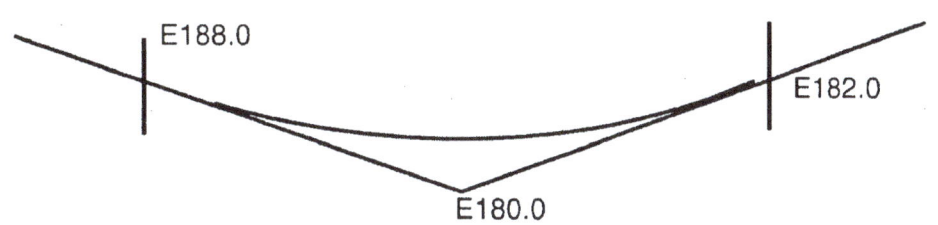

   The above sketch shows a parabolic vertical curve. The tangents are of equal length. The elevation of the center of the curve is

   A. 85.0   B. 84.5   C. 83.5   D. 82.5

   2._____

3. The volume of the solid shown below is in cubic inches, *most nearly*

   A. 42   B. 40   C. 38   D. 36

   3._____

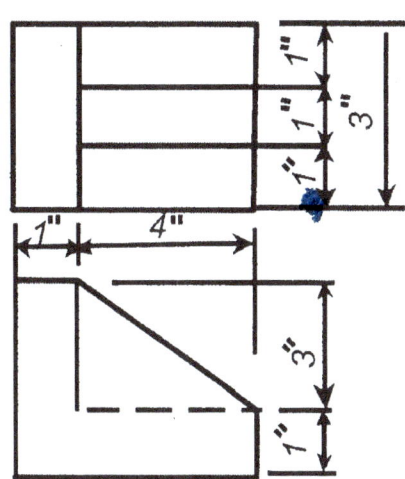

4. The volume of the solid shown below is, *most nearly*, 4.____

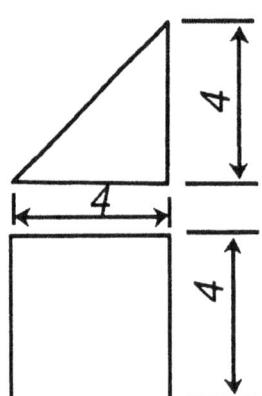

A. 64 B. 32 C. $32\sqrt{2}$ D. $16\sqrt{2}$

5. In trigonometry, the expression $1-2\sin^2 x$ is equal to 5.____

A. sin 2 x B. cos 2 x C. sin 1/2 x D. cos 1/2 x

6. A survey was made of a five-sided piece of property as shown below. Four of the angles were measured as noted on the diagram. 6.____
The fifth should be in degrees, *most nearly*,

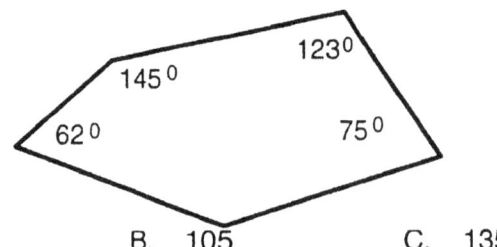

A. 45 B. 105 C. 135 D. 35

7. The diagonal of a square is $\sqrt{72}$. 7.____

The area of the square is, in square feet, *most nearly*,

A. 36 B. 48 C. 64 D. 72

8. A square whose side is *a* has the same area as a rectangle whose sides are *b* and *c*. 8.____
Of the following statements, the one that is TRUE is

A. $a = \sqrt{bc}$ B. $b = ac$ C. $b = \sqrt{ac}$ D. $ab = bc$

9. The mathematical formula that will give the MOST accurate results in determining the area of an irregular plane surface is: 9.____

A. Simpson's Rule B. Horizontal Rule
C. Pappus' Theorum D. Average End Area Method

10. If $y = x^3$, $\dfrac{d^2y}{dx^2}$ is equal to

    A. 6x   B. $3x^2$ C. $\dfrac{x^5}{20}$ D. $2x^3$

11. The most probable value of a series of measurements of the same quantity made under similar conditions is the arithmetic mean of the quantity. A line was measured four times and the recorded lengths of the line are: 913.35, 913.36, 913.42, 913.43.
    The MOST probable length of the line is

    A. 913.36   B. 913.38   C. 913.39   D. 913.40

12. The bearing of line C D in the traverse shown below is

    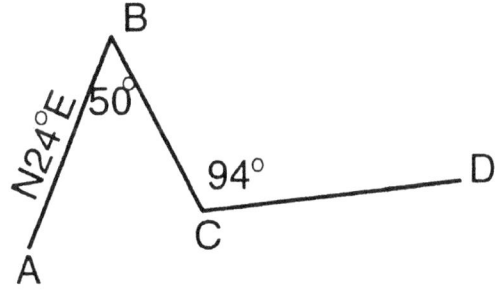

    A. N 78°E   B. N 68°E   C. S 26°E   D. N 78°W

13. The stadia method is commonly used in _____ surveys.

    A. topographic   B. triangulation
    C. photogrammetric   D. geodetic

14. A surveyor is assigned to check the structural steel of a tall steel frame building. The steel is past the first floor.
    Of the following, the MOST important factor to be checked is the _____ of the _____ columns.

    A. plumbness; interior   B. plumbness; exterior
    C. elevation; interior   D. elevation; exterior

15. It is necessary to plot a circular curve on a drawing. If the radius or center is not known, the number of points on the circumference needed to determine the curve is

    A. 1   B. 2   C. 3   D. 4

16. In ordinary profile leveling, there

    A. are more foresights than backsights
    B. are more backsights than foresights
    C. are as many foresights as backsights
    D. may be more or less foresights than backsights

17.

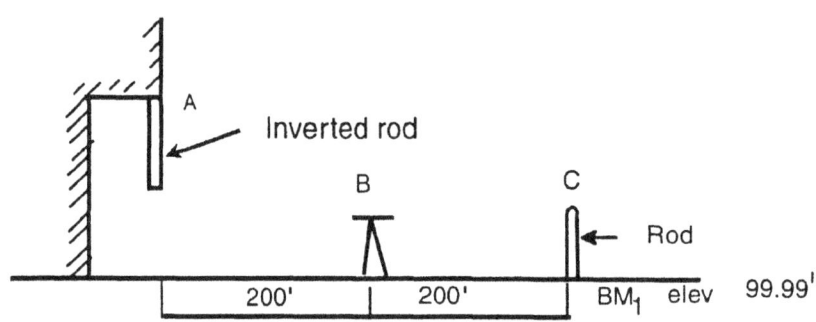

The rod reading at C = 4.39', and the rod reading at A = 4.39'. The elevation of point A is

A. 99.99' B. 108.77' C. 4.39' D. 104.38'

18. The coordinates of point A are (N 780, E 660) and the coordinates of point B are (N 650, E 620). Point B is _____ of A.

A. Northeast
B. Northwest
C. Southeast
D. Southwest

19. The following set of notes was taken on the closed level circuit EFG. The elevation of bench mark E is 35.47. There are no errors in levelling.

Sta	BS	HI	FS	Elev.
E	6.29			35.47
F	4.20		5.05	
G	3.21		6.02	
F				
E				

The elevation of BMG is
A. 42.73 B. 34.89 C. 43.15 D. 38.10

20. If the bench mark elevation is 6.42 and the B. S. reading is 5.50, the reading that should be set on the rod as an F. S. reading to set an elevation of 8.23 is in feet, *most nearly,*

A. 3.69 B. 7.31 C. 9.15 D. 11.92

21. When transferring line and grade from the surface to a deep tunnel,

A. a small error in transferring grade to the bottom of the shaft will cause a large error in grade in the tunnel
B. a small error in transferring line to the bottom of the shaft will cause a large error in line in the tunnel
C. trigonometric leveling is used to transfer grade into the tunnel
D. reciprocal leveling is used to transfer grade into the tunnel

22. The invert of a sewer is a (the)

A. syphon
B. bottom of the outside surface
C. bottom of the inside surface
D. top of the inside surface

23. The datum in one borough is 1.725' above mean sea level. The elevation of a point in the borough is minus 2.50. The datum in another borough is 2.725' above mean sea level. The elevation of the point with reference to the latter datum is

   A. -4.225   B. -3.225   C. 1.50   D. -3.50

24.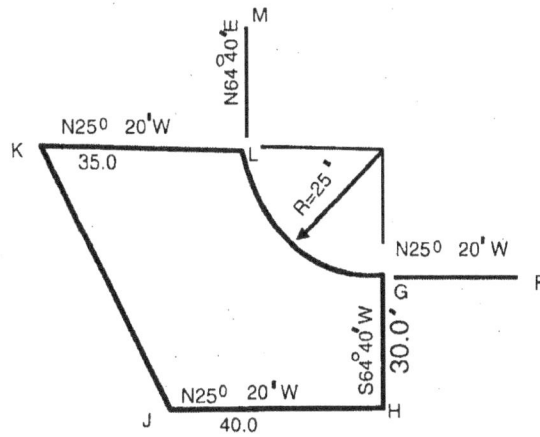

The area of the enclosed figure is, in square feet, *most nearly,*
   A. 2100   B. 2260   C. 2370   D. 2450

25. The sin $(x + 60°)$ is equal to

   A. $\sin(30 - x)$
   C. $\cos(30 - x)$
   B. $\sin(30 + x)$
   D. $\cos(30 + x)$

KEY (CORRECT ANSWERS)

1. C   11. C
2. D   12. B
3. D   13. A
4. B   14. B
5. B   15. C

6. C   16. A
7. A   17. B
8. A   18. D
9. A   19. B
10. A   20. A

21. B
22. C
23. D
24. B
25. C

TEST 2

DIRECTIONS: Each question or incomplete statement is followed by several suggested answers or completions. Select the one that BEST answers the question or completes the Statement. *PRINT THE LETTER OF THE CORRECT ANSWER IN THE SPACE AT THE RIGHT.*

1. The shape of the main cables on a suspension bridge is, *most nearly,* a(n)   1.____
   A. parabola
   B. hyperbola
   C. circular segment
   D. straight line

2. The area of a rectangular plot that scales 3" x 4 1/2" on a map whose scale is 1" =60' is, in square feet, *most nearly,*   2.____
   A. 13 1/2
   B. 48,600
   C. 810
   D. 720

3. To a water tank that is 1/4 full, 250 gallons of water are added. The tank, then, is 1/3 full. The capacity of the tank is, in gallons, *most nearly,*   3.____
   A. 12,000
   B. 3,000
   C. 1,000
   D. 750

4. A random line is used in surveying when   4.____
   A. it is desired to connect two distant points with a straight line when the points are not intervisible
   B. a trial line is needed to determine the best method of running a survey
   C. it is necessary to set the transit on line
   D. the actual distance between two points is too great to be sighted from one end of the line

5. Of the following numbers, the one that is NOT a rational number is   5.____
   A. -1 5/8
   B. i^2
   C. $\sqrt{2}$
   D. 0

6. If the magnetic declination is 12°W, and the magnetic bearing of a line is N34°E, then the *true bearing* of the line is   6.____
   A. N58° E
   B. N46° E
   C. N22° E
   D. N10° E

7. (5+3i) (5-3i) is   7.____
   A. 34
   B. 25-9i
   C. $25-6i-9i^2$
   D. 16

8. $\cos^2 x = 1/2$. x equals, in degrees   8.____
   A. 15
   B. 30
   C. 45
   D. 60

9. The deflection angle required to lay out a 50-foot chord of a 3°00' circular curve is, *most nearly,*   9.____
   A. 0°45'
   B. 1°30'
   C. 2°15'
   D. 3°00'

10.

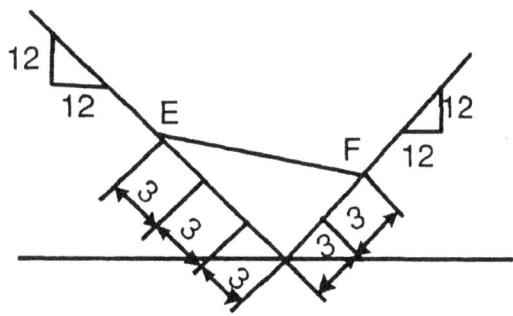

Distance EF is, in inches, *most nearly*,
A. 10 7/16   B. 10 9/16   C. 10 4/16   D. 10 13/16

11. If in the binary system of notation,
$$1 = 1$$
$$2 = 10$$
$$3 = 11,$$
the number six would be represented in the binary system by the number

A. 100   B. 101   C. 110   D. 11

12. The *third* term in the expansion $(a+b)^6$ is

A. $15a^4b^2$ B. $20a^4b^2$ C. $30a^4b^2$ D. $10a^4b^2$

13. 48 x 12 is equal to

A. $3^3 \cdot 4^2$ B. $4^3 \cdot 3^2$ C. $4^4 \cdot 3^2$ D. $3^4 \cdot 4^2$

14. For a given angle *x*, which of the following is CORRECT?

A. $\tan^2 x = 1 + \sec^2 x$
B. $\sin^2 x + \cos^2 x = 1$
C. $\tan x = \dfrac{\cos x}{\sin x}$
D. $\sec x = \dfrac{1}{\sin x}$

15. If $x = 1$ and $x^3 + x^2 + x^1 + x + x^{-1} = y$, y equals

A. 2   B. 3   C. 4   D. 5

16. A specification for a heavy construction job reads, in part: All timber used for sheeting, shoring, bracing or other temporary purposes shall be sound and free from any defects that may impair its strength.
According to good practice, the method by which the above provision is enforced is that the engineer in charge or an assigned inspector

A. sees that the appropriate grade stamp appears on each piece
B. checks for compliance by visual inspection of the lumber used
C. prohibits use of previously used lumber
D. reports the defects to the materials inspection division for a ruling

3 (#2)

17. When a membrane waterproofing is referred to, it means the   17.____
    A. adding of a waterproofing ingredient to the fresh concrete
    B. thorough draining of the foundation
    C. coating of the structure with waterproof material
    D. using of a dense concrete mix

18. The welding symbol ⟋▽ designates a _____ weld.   18.____

    A. fillet   B. butt
    C. spot   D. plug

19.   19.____

    The value of the weight W is, in pounds, *most nearly*,
    A. 800   B. 850   C. 900   D. 950

20. A squad leader on design work in the office should assign work to the members of his group so that   20.____

    A. each member will get the work he likes best to do
    B. one group will usually prepare designs and another group will usually check
    C. older members of the group will get the more difficult assignments
    D. each member of the group will get the work for which he is best suited

21. Water flowing into the top of a tank from pipe A can fill the tank in 4 minutes. Water from pipe B alone can fill the tank in 6 minutes.   21.____
    If both pipes are used, the time in which the tank will be filled is, in minutes, *most nearly*,

    A. 2.0   B. 2.8   C. 2.6   D. 2.4

22. Vermiculite is used as an aggregate in plaster PRIMARILY because of its   22.____

    A. quicksetting characteristics
    B. light weight
    C. workability
    D. low cost

23. In the formula, $H_f = f \dfrac{1}{d} \dfrac{v^2}{2g}$ the value of f for smooth cast iron pipes, is, *most nearly*,   23.____

    A. 0.02   B. 1.486   C. 0.14   D. 100.0

24. Drop manholes are 24.____
    A. sometimes used when streets have steep slopes
    B. never used in an original sewer design
    C. not used in flat topography
    D. usually shallower than regular manholes

25. In a unit price contract, 25.____
    A. payment to the contractor is based upon the total quantities of the various items comprising the work
    B. the agreement stipulates a specified sum to cover the cost of the entire job
    C. payment is based on the Engineer News-Record construction costs index
    D. contractor is required to furnish labor and material bills to establish the cost of the job

---

KEY (CORRECT ANSWERS)

1.	A	11.	C
2.	B	12.	A
3.	B	13.	B
4.	A	14.	B
5.	C	15.	D
6.	C	16.	B
7.	A	17.	C
8.	C	18.	A
9.	A	19.	C
10.	D	20.	D

21. D
22. B
23. A
24. A
25. A

EXAMINATION SECTION
TEST 1

DIRECTIONS: Each question or incomplete statement is followed by several suggested answers or completions. Select the one that BEST answers the question or completes the statement. *PRINT THE LETTER OF THE CORRECT ANSWER IN THE SPACE AT THE RIGHT.*

1. A general contractor, on a lump sum building construction job, is required to submit a breakdown of his estimate in order to

    A. prevent collusion in bidding
    B. serve as a guide in checking his monthly estimates for payment
    C. enable designers to prepare budget estimates for proposed work
    D. enable designers to compare it with their estimate of cost of the job

    1.____

2. Of the following, the index MOST often applied to indicate the strength of sewage is

    A. odor
    B. biochemical oxygen demand
    C. foaming
    D. turbidity

    2.____

3. Of the following, the MINIMUM amount of cover required for water mains in the city is *primarily* determined by the

    A. traffic shock loads
    B. pressure in the main
    C. depth of rock below street surfaces
    D. depth of frost

    3.____

4. The one of the following in which an inspector of pile driving has the MOST interest during driving wood piles is

    A. weather conditions
    B. mushrooming of the head
    C. penetration
    D. water table location

    4.____

5. A bidder on a public job is required to furnish a bid bond to guarantee that he will

    A. sign a contract if awarded the job
    B. complete the job on schedule
    C. pay the mechanics who will work on the job
    D. pay the subcontractors whom he will employ to work on the job

    5.____

Questions 6-7.

DIRECTIONS: Questions 6 and 7 refer to the following diagram.

A section through a roof appears as shown below.

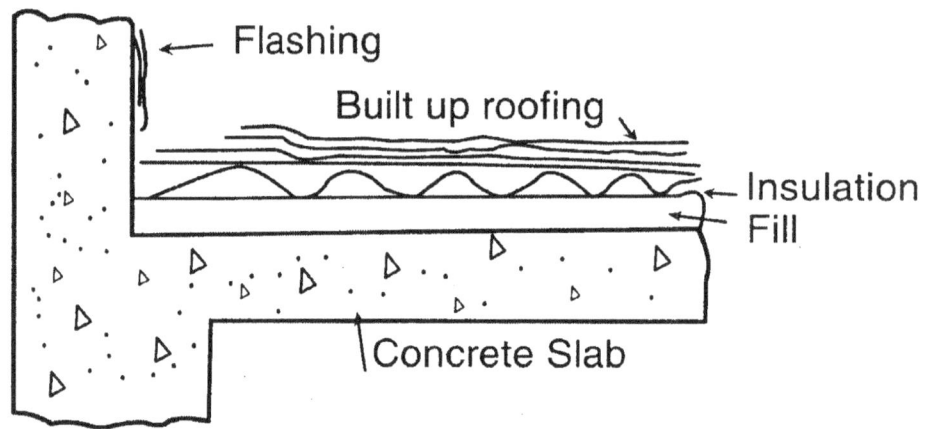

6. Of the following, the MAIN purpose of the fill is to

   A. provide a smooth base for the insulation
   B. reduce sound transmission
   C. absorb impact of roof loads
   D. facilitate drainage

7. Of the following, the material composition of the fill is *most likely*

   A. one-inch cinder block
   B. compacted sand
   C. Wood
   D. lightweight concrete

8. An excavation for a building in the downtown area is kept dry by pumping from a sump. It would be a danger signal to an inspector if

   A. the pumped water is always clear
   B. after a heavy rain, the pumped water is muddy
   C. the pumped water is continually muddy
   D. the rate of pumping decreases materially with time

9. The PRIMARY reason for placing reinforced steel in concrete is that concrete is weak in

   A. torsion   B. tension   C. compression   D. bond

10. Of the following types of construction, the one that would *most likely* be paid for on a lump sum basis would be a new

    A. subway
    B. sewer
    C. street paving and regulating
    D. building

11. Of the following situations, the one in which it is MOST important to have a fire extinguisher on hand is when

    A. welding a broken bracket on a bulldozer
    B. welding a structural steel field connection
    C. burning reinforcing steel in place before a concrete pour
    D. bending reinforced steel at the bar bending machine

12. Wall plaster is composed of

    A. sand, cement, gypsum, water
    B. coarse aggregate, gypsum, water
    C. sand, gypsum, water
    D. lime, gypsum, cement, water

13. Of the following, the LEAST important factor in establishing grades for a new urban street is existing

    A. manholes   B. underground utilities
    C. sewers   D. sidewalks

14. The activated sludge treatment process reduces organic matter in the sewage to inorganic matter PRIMARILY by

    A. electrolysis   B. sedimentation
    C. bacteriological action D. catalytic action

15. Assume that you are a party chief on a preliminary survey for a major construction project with a four-man party. Two of your men are able to operate the transit. You consider one of these men an expert, while the other is lacking in experience. You have been following a policy of assigning each man to the transit on alternate days. You get a call from the design department to furnish a check on a series of angles as quickly as possible. On this day, it is the inexperienced man's turn at the transit. You should

    A. allow the inexperienced man to run the gun for that is the only way he can become experienced
    B. have the experienced man run the gun and explain the need for speed and accuracy
    C. run the gun yourself to avoid arguments
    D. have the experienced man run the gun and explain to the Inexperienced man that the next time the design department wants a quick check, it would be his turn at the transit

16. A Rockwell test is a test for

    A. water hardness   B. well water purity
    C. hardness of metal   D. rock bearing capacity

17. A slump test is made on a sample of concrete PRIMARILY to measure its

    A. finishing qualities B. resistance to bleeding
    C. strength   D. workability

18. Of the following, the MOST important factor that the individual must fulfill in order to insure his own safety on a construction job is to

    A. be familiar with the specifications
    B. work slowly
    C. be alert
    D. wear clothing to suit the climatic condition

KEY (CORRECT ANSWERS)

1. B
2. B
3. D
4. C
5. A

6. D
7. D
8. C
9. B
10. D

11. C
12. C
13. A
14. C
15. B

16. C
17. D
18. C
19. C
20. D

21. A
22. D
23. B
24. D
25. A

TEST 2

DIRECTIONS: Each question or incomplete statement is followed by several suggested answers or completions. Select the one that BEST answers the question or completes the statement. *PRINT THE LETTER OF THE CORRECT ANSWER IN THE SPACE AT THE RIGHT.*

1. Of the following, the one which is NOT usually used for primary treatment of sewage is a

   A. comminutor
   B. grit chamber
   C. trickling filter
   D. skimming

   1._____

2. Of the following, construction joints in reinforced concrete floor systems should be made at

   A. the edge of a beam
   B. the edge of a girder
   C. points of maximum shear
   D. points of maximum positive bending moment

   2._____

3. To prevent objectionable deposits in a sanitary sewer, the MINIMUM average velocity when flowing full should be, in fps,

   A. 0.5   B. 1.2   C. 2.0   D. 3.0

   3._____

4. The tool that is GENERALLY used in plaster work to float over freshly rodded brown mortar is

   A. darby   B. featheredge   C. paddle   D. rod

   4._____

5. An inferior paint well applied to a thoroughly cleaned and conditioned surface will give many times the protection and decorative effect that will be obtained by the best paint poorly applied to an uncleaned or damp surface.
   Assuming that the above evaluation is correct, an APPROPRIATE instruction for your painting inspector, based on this statement, is

   A. to make sure that the paint used is equivalent to the approved sample
   B. to allow use of inferior paint provided the surface is clean and dry
   C. that the inspection of cleaning and painting of all surfaces is too casual
   D. to make sure the surface to be painted is clean and free from dampness

   5._____

6. Of the following, the MOST compressible soil is usually

   A. sand   B. clay   C. gravel   D. silt

   6._____

7. Vitrified clay pipe

   A. can be ordered in lengths from 4 to 16 feet
   B. is easy to cut
   C. is joined by the use of Dresser Couplings
   D. is hard and brittle

   7._____

8. A *hawk* is a tool USUALLY used in

   A. plastering
   B. brickwork
   C. roofing
   D. carpentry

   8._____

9. The specifications for concrete state that the water used for concrete shall be free of organic material.
Of the following chemicals, the one that is organic is

   A. NaCl B. $C_6H_{12}O_6$ C. HNO_3 D. $CaSO_4 2H_2O$

10. The *Proctor Test* is used in testing

    A. asphalt B. concrete C. soils D. mortar

11. A rectangular reinforced concrete beam is to resist a bending moment of 75,000 pound-feet.
If the effective depth is 20' and K $(= \frac{1}{2}f_c jk)$ is 180, the required width of the beam, in inches, is MOST NEARLY (M=Kbd^2)

    A. 12.3 B. 12.5 C. 12.7 D. 12.9

12. Of the following, the Chezy Formula, in reference to the flow of water, is used to compute the

    A. velocity B. viscosity C. pressure D. losses

13. The length of a 20-penny nail is MOST NEARLY _____ inches.

    A. $2\frac{1}{2}$ B. 3 C. $3\frac{1}{2}$ D. 4

14. In the schedule of room finishes on an architectural plan of a building are the headings: Room, Space No., Floor, Base, Wall, Ceiling.
The Base *most likely* refers to the

    A. wainscot
    B. material beneath the flooring material such as felt or paper
    C. material at the bottom of the wall
    D. structural material supporting the floor

15. Of the following, the STRONGEST and MOST DURABLE of all building stones used to face an exterior wall is

    A. trap B. granite C. limestone D. sandstone

16. The width and thickness of the main plate of a riveted lap joint is 6" and 3/4", respectively. The allowable loads in shear, bearing, and tension are 70,000#, 80,000#, and 60,000#, respectively. The allowable f_s = 20000 psi.
The efficiency of this joint is MOST NEARLY

    A. 82% B. 55% C. 75% D. 66.7%

17. A post, consisting of a steel pipe whose net cross-sectional area is 40 sq. inches, is subjected to direct compression by a load of 80,000#.
If the post is 8 ft. high, the reduction in length due to the load is, in inches, MOST NEARLY (E= 30,000,000#/sq. in. and $E = \frac{S}{E}$)

    A. .001 B. .006 C. .011 D. .016

18.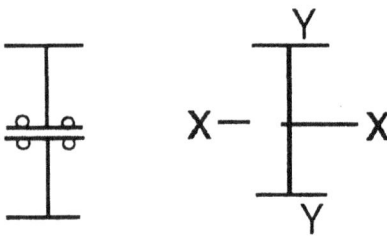

DATA:
14 WF 68 depth = 14 in.
width = 10 in.
area = 20 sq. in
I_{xx} = 724"⁴
I_{yy} = 121"⁴
$r = \sqrt{I/A}$

Two WF 68 columns are connected as shown above.
Their LEAST radius of gyration when acting together as a unit is in inches, MOST NEARLY

A. 2.46   B. 4.92   C. 6.02   D. 12.04

19. The PRIMARY physical difference between steel and cast iron is that steel is much

A. *lighter* than cast iron
B. *weaker* in compression
C. *stronger* in tension
D. *weaker* in tension

20. Of the following, the one that is an example of a flexible pavement is a

A. gravel base and a concrete wearing course
B. plain concrete slab
C. gravel base and a bituminous wearing course
D. concrete base and an asphalt wearing course

21. Shutoff valves on 12" water supply lines found in the city streets USUALLY are _____ valves.

A. gate   B. globe   C. check   D. stop

22. An analysis of drinking water shows that the pH is 6.0. The pH may be increased by adding

A. H_2SO_4
B. chlorine
C. caustic soda
D. fluorine

23.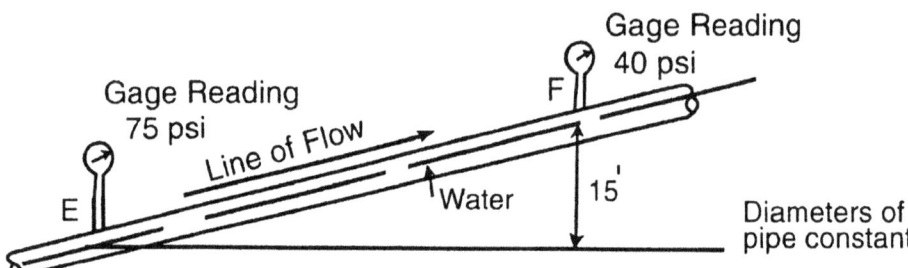

The head loss between E and F is, in feet of water, MOST NEARLY

A. 66   B. 81   C. 90   D. 93

24. A contract for a new building is generally broken into four separate contracts. 24._____
These contracts are USUALLY:

   A. General Construction, Plumbing & Drainage, Heating and Ventilating, Electrical
   B. Foundation, Superstructure, Electrical, Mechanical
   C. Structural, Mechanical, Electrical, Foundation
   D. General Construction, Plumbing, Drainage, Electrical

25. The terms *shakes, checks, seasoning,* and *preservation* are all likely to be used in specifications for 25._____

   A. glass brick
   B. cast iron
   C. plaster
   D. timber

KEY (CORRECT ANSWERS)

1.	C	11.	B
2.	D	12.	A
3.	C	13.	D
4.	A	14.	C
5.	D	15.	B
6.	B	16.	D
7.	D	17.	B
8.	A	18.	A
9.	B	19.	C
10.	C	20.	C

21. A
22. C
23. A
24. A
25. D

EXAMINATION SECTION
TEST 1

DIRECTIONS: Each question or incomplete statement is followed by several suggested answers or completions. Select the one that BEST answers the question or completes the statement. *PRINT THE LETTER OF THE CORRECT ANSWER IN THE SPACE AT THE RIGHT.*

1. The ultimate strength of a short 16" x 16" concrete column with 8 #8 steel bars with f_c = 4000 psi and f_y = 69000 psi is, in kips, MOST NEARLY
   A. 1290   B. 1320   C. 1350   D. 1380

2. Transverse ties with the vertical steel #10 bars or smaller have a minimum size of _____ bar.
   A. #2   B. #3   C. #4   D. #5

3. The capacity reduction, ϕ, for shear on a concrete beam section is
   A. .75   B. .80   C. .85   D. .90

4. The balanced steel ratio occurs when the steel
   A. and concrete fail simultaneously
   B. fails before the concrete
   C. fails after the concrete
   D. reaches its ultimate strength

5. The minimum requirement of $p = \frac{200}{f_y}$ is necessary in concrete beam design to insure that the
   A. concrete will not fail before the reinforcing steel
   B. member does not lose strength when it first cracks
   C. bonding between steel and concrete does not fail
   D. deflection of the beam is not excessive

6. In ultimate strength design, the ϕ value for flexure without axial load is the largest of all ϕ factors because
   A. the loads are less variable in bending than they are for axial loads
   B. there is more variability in shear loads than in bending moments
   C. steel has a greater coefficient of expansion than concrete
   D. there is less variability in steel strength than in concrete strength

7. If, in the design of a reinforced concrete beam section, the service moment is 40 k-ft. for dead load and 90 k-ft. for live load, the load factored moment is, in kip feet, MOST NEARLY (ϕ is not included)
   A. 190   B. 209   C. 219   D. 229

Questions 8-12.

DIRECTIONS: Questions 8 through 12, inclusive, refer to the reinforced concrete beam section shown below.

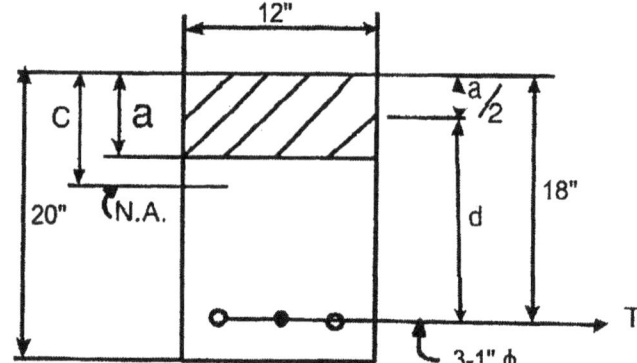

$f_c = 4000\#/\square'$

$f_y = 60,000 \#/\square"$

Area of $1" \phi = .79\square"$

8. The proportion of steel to concrete, p, is MOST NEARLY
   A. .011   B. .010   C. .009   D. .008

9. The maximum value of T, in kips, is MOST NEARLY
   A. 138   B. 142   C. 146   D. 150

10. The value of a corresponding to the maximum value of T is, in inches, MOST NEARLY
    A. 3.5   B. 3.8   C. 4.2   D. 4.6

11. The moment, in foot kips, that the beam section can carry, assuming $\phi = 0.9$, is, in foot kips, MOST NEARLY
    A. 173   B. 178   C. 183   D. 188

12. The value of c is, in inches, MOST NEARLY
    A. 3.7   B. 3.9   C. 4.1   D. 4.3

13. Granite is the type of rock that is
    A. silicious
    B. igneous
    C. sedimentary
    D. metamorphic

14. In a trial batch of concrete, the fine aggregate has a weight of 148 pounds. It has 6% of its weight in water. The specific gravity of the fine aggregate is 2.65.
    The absolute volume of the fine aggregate, in cubic feet, is MOST NEARLY
    A. .84   B. .82   C. .80   D. .78

15. The optimum concrete mix for a given structural element having a given water-cement ratio would have a
    A. maximum allowable size of coarse aggregate and a minimum allowable slump
    B. minimum allowable size of coarse aggregate and a minimum amount of slump

C. maximum allowable size of coarse aggregate and a maximum allowable slump
D. minimum size of coarse aggregate and a maximum slump

16. Bulking of sand
    A. varies inversely with the water content
    B. is greater with coarse sand than with fine sand
    C. decreases when there is high moisture in the atmosphere
    D. is a maximum when the water content is about 6% by weight

17. A medium-curing cutback asphalt would MOST likely contain as a solvent
    A. gasoline   B. naphtha
    C. an oil of low volatility   D. kerosene

18. The PRIMARY reason for using cutback asphalt is that it
    A. gives a harder riding surface
    B. is more resistant to softening at high outdoor temperatures
    C. requires little or no heat during placing
    D. does not age as rapidly as ordinary asphalt

19. Emulsified asphalt is an emulsion primarily of asphalt and
    A. toluene   B. water   C. kerosene   D. naphtha

Questions 20-22.

DIRECTIONS: Questions 20 through 22 are to be answered on the basis of the 400' vertical curve shown below.

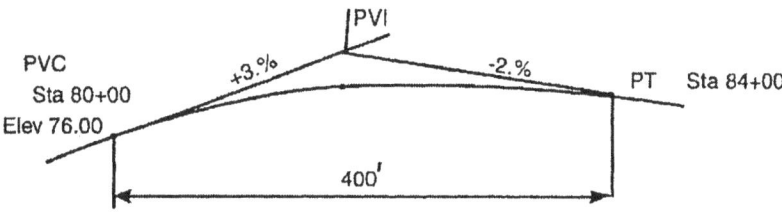

20. The elevation of the vertical curve at Sta 82+00 is, in feet, MOST NEARLY
    A. 79.25   B. 79.50   C. 79.75   D. 80.00

21. The station at the high point of the vertical curve is MOST NEARLY
    A. 82+20   B. 82+40   C. 82+60   D. 82+80

22. The elevation of the high point of the vertical curve is, in feet, MOST NEARLY
    A. 79.60   B. 79.70   C. 79.80   D. 79.90

23. If a 1° central angle of a circle intercepts an arc of 100', the radius of the circle is, in feet, MOST NEARLY
    A. 5709   B. 5729   C. 5749   5769

24. A circular horizontal curve has a radius of 1600' and a tangent length of 950'. The length of the curve from PC to PT is, in feet, MOST NEARLY
A. 1714.6   B. 1724.6   C. 1734.6   D. 1744.6

25.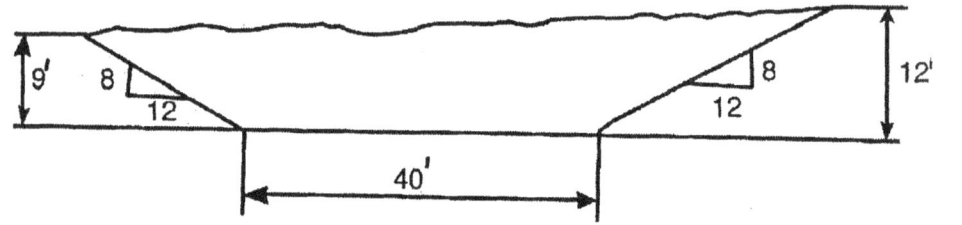

The cross-section of an area in cut in a highway excavation is shown above. the area of the cut is, in square feet, MOST NEARLY
A. 562   B. 582   C. 602   D. 622

KEY (CORRECT ANSWERS)

1. B		11. A	
2. B		12. C	
3. C		13. B	
4. A		14. A	
5. B		15. A	
6. D		16. D	
7. B		17. D	
8. A		18. C	
9. B		19. B	
10. A		20. B	

21. B
22. A
23. B
24. A
25. A

TEST 2

DIRECTIONS: Each question or incomplete statement is followed by several suggested answers or completions. Select the one that BEST answers the question or completes the statement. *PRINT THE LETTER OF THE CORRECT ANSWER IN THE SPACE AT THE RIGHT.*

1. The water pressure in the pipe as shown by the manometer at the right is, in pounds per square inch, MOST NEARLY
   A. 5.5
   B. 5.9
   C. 6.3
   D. 6.7

   1.____

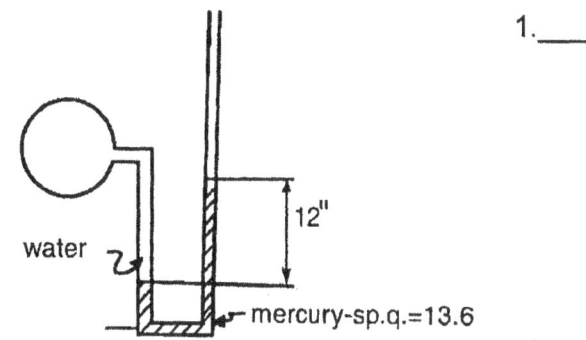

2. The theoretical discharge over a rectangular weir of length L is $Q = cL\sqrt{2qHx}$, where x is
   A. ½   B. 1   C. ³/₂   D. 2

   2.____

3. If one cubic foot of water per second under a head of 80' is delivered to a turbine, the horsepower that the turbine can deliver, assuming no losses, is
   A. 5   B. 7   C. 9   D. 11

   3.____

Questions 4-5.

DIRECTIONS: Questions 4 and 5 are to be answered on the basis of the diagram below of the 3" outlet from a tank of water.

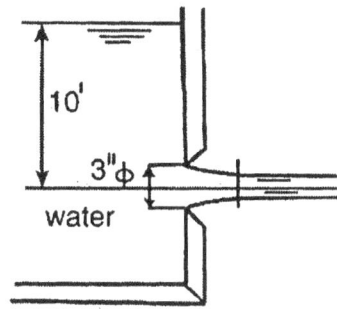

4. The velocity of the water at the point of discharge is, in feet per second, MOST NEARLY
   A. 22   B. 25   C. 28   D. 30

   4.____

5. The discharge rate, in cubic feet per second, is MOST NEARLY
   A. .50   B. .75   C. 1.00   D. 1.25

   5.____

25

6. When a sewer is built using vitrified clay pipe, construction starts from the _____ elevation with the bell facing _____.
   A. highest; downward
   B. highest; upward
   C. lowest; downward
   D. lowest; upward

7. A sewer that runs along a waterfront and carries sewage into a sewage treatment plant is known as a(n) _____ sewer.
   A. outfall B. intercepting C. relief D. combined

8. The change in temperature, in degrees Fahrenheit, that will cause a 100 foot steel tape to lengthen .01 feet is MOST NEARLY
   A. 5 B. 10 C. 15 D. 20

9. A map is drawn to a scale of 1 inch equals 200 feet. Contours are drawn at intervals of 2 feet.
   If the distance between two adjacent contours measures ½ inch, the slope of the surface is MOST NEARLY
   A. 2% B. 3% C. 4% D. 5%

10. The angle ϕ at E caused by a moment M at E is
    A. $\dfrac{ML}{EI}$
    B. $\dfrac{ML}{2EI}$
    C. $\dfrac{ML}{3EI}$
    D. $\dfrac{ML}{4EI}$

Questions 11-12.

DIRECTIONS: Questions 11 and 12 are to be answered on the basis of the following diagram.

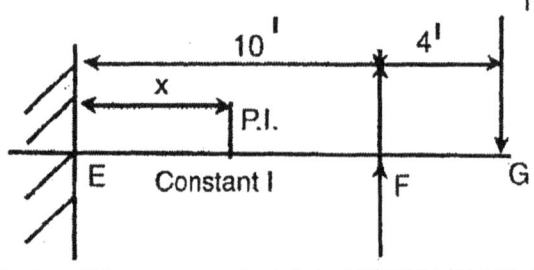

11. The magnitude of the moment at E is MOST NEARLY
    A. 20^{lk} B. 23^{lk} C. 27^{lk} D. 30^{lk}

12. The vertical reaction at E is, in kips, MOST NEARLY _____ downward.
    A. 6^K B. 5^K C. 4^K D. 3^K

13. The distance x from the point E to the point of inflection is, in feet, MOST NEARLY 13.____
    A. 4.33 B. 4.00 C. 3.67 D. 3.33

Questions 14-15.

DIRECTIONS: Questions 14 and 15 are to be answered on the basis of the cantilever beam shown below.

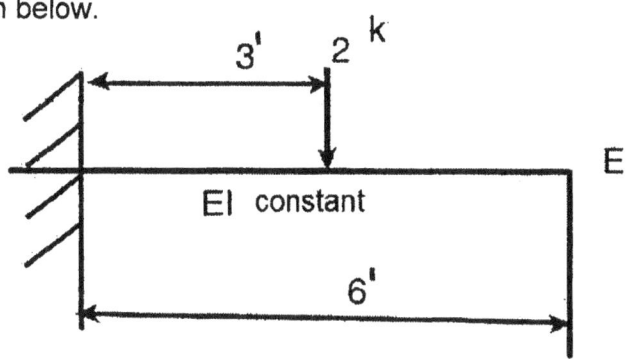

14. The deflection at the end E of the cantilever beam shown above is 14.____
    A. $30^{k13/EI}$ B. $34^{k13/EI}$ C. $40^{k13/EI}$ D. $45^{k13/EI}$

15. The slope of the beam at E is 15.____
    A. $6^{k12/EI}$ B. $9^{k12/EI}$ C. $12^{k12/EI}$ D. $15^{k12/EI}$

16. With both ends of the beam EF fixed, the magnitude of the fixed end moment at E is, in foot-kips, 16.____
    A. 18
    B. 21
    C. 24
    D. 270

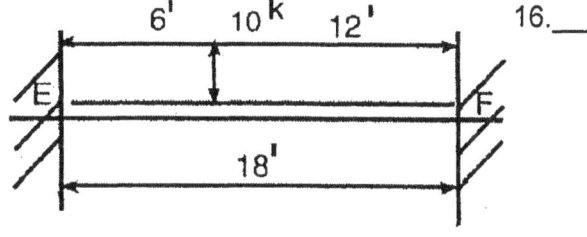

17. The conjugate beam for the beam shown at the right would be 17.____

18. The deflection at the center of the beam shown at the right is
   A. $\dfrac{PL^3}{16EI}$
   B. $\dfrac{PL^3}{32EI}$
   C. $\dfrac{PL^3}{48EI}$
   D. $\dfrac{PL^3}{64EI}$

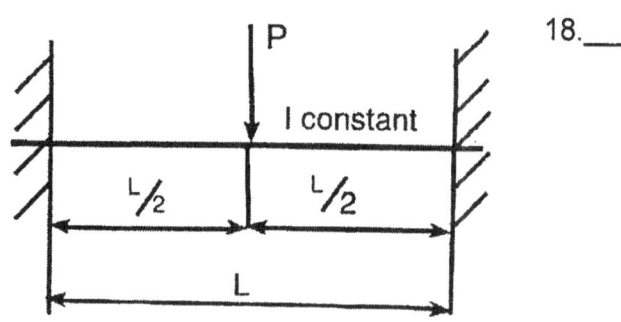

19. The deflection at the center of the beam shown at the right is
   A. $\dfrac{PL^3}{48EI}$
   B. $\dfrac{PL^3}{96EI}$
   C. $\dfrac{PL^3}{192EI}$
   D. $\dfrac{PL^3}{184EI}$

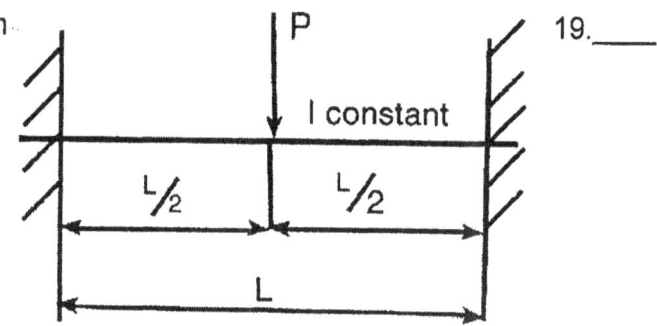

20. The offset deflection on the fixed end beam in terms of L, M, E, and I is
   A. $\dfrac{ML^2}{6EI}$
   B. $\dfrac{ML^2}{8EI}$
   C. $\dfrac{ML^2}{10EI}$
   D. $\dfrac{ML^2}{12EI}$

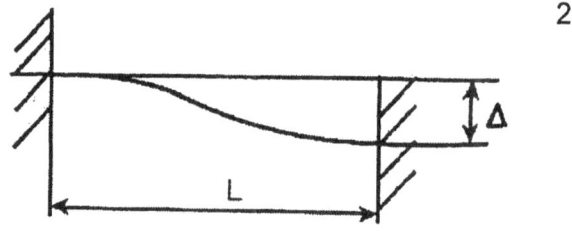

21. If the deflection on a beam is $\dfrac{KPL^3}{EI}$, where K is dimensionless, L is in feet, P is in kips, E is in kips per square inch, and I is in inches⁴, the constant that the resulting product must be multiplied by in order to have the deflection in inches is
   A. 12
   B. 12^2
   C. 12^3
   D. 12^4

22. The maximum moment on the beam shown at the right, in foot-kips, is
   A. 16.5
   B. 18.5
   C. 20.5
   D. 22.5

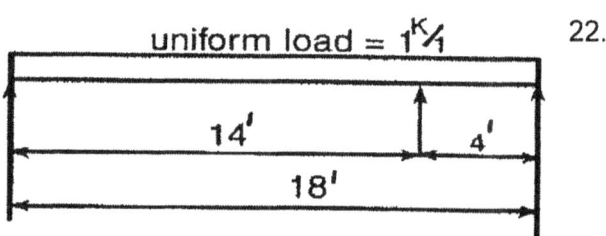

Questions 23-24.

DIRECTIONS: Questions 23 and 24 are to be answered on the basis of the beam EF shown below with a triangular loading.

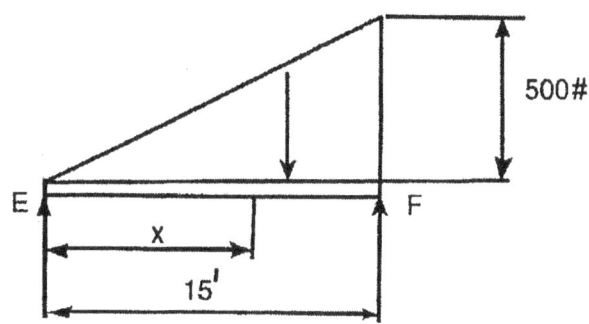

23. The distance x to the point of shears is, in feet, MOST NEARLY 23._____
    A. 8.00   B. 8.33   C. 8.66   D. 9.00

24. The maximum moment on the beam is, in foot-kips, MOST NEARLY 24._____
    A. 6.82   B. 7.22   C. 7.62   D. 8.03

25. The change in length of member EF due to the 10000 pound loads is, in inches, MOST NEARLY 25._____
    A. .032
    B. .043
    C. .056
    D. .067

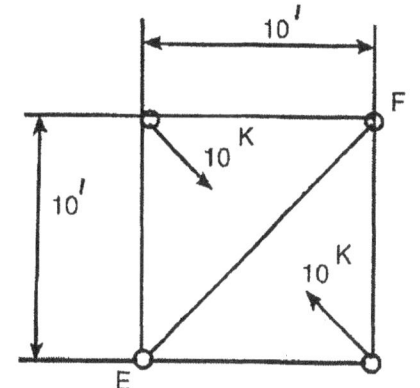

$E = 30,000 K/\square"$
Cross-section area of EF = 1 square inch

KEY (CORRECT ANSWERS)

1.	A		11.	A
2.	C		12.	A
3.	C		13.	D
4.	B		14.	D
5.	B		15.	B
6.	D		16.	D
7.	B		17.	D
8.	C		18.	C
9.	A		19.	C
10.	C		20.	A

21. C
22. C
23. C
24. B
25. C

TEST 3

DIRECTIONS: Each question or incomplete statement is followed by several suggested answers or completions. Select the one that BEST answers the question or completes the statement. *PRINT THE LETTER OF THE CORRECT ANSWER IN THE SPACE AT THE RIGHT.*

Questions 1-5.

DIRECTIONS: Questions 1 through 5, inclusive, are to be answered on the basis of the bent with rigid connections at E, F, G, and H.

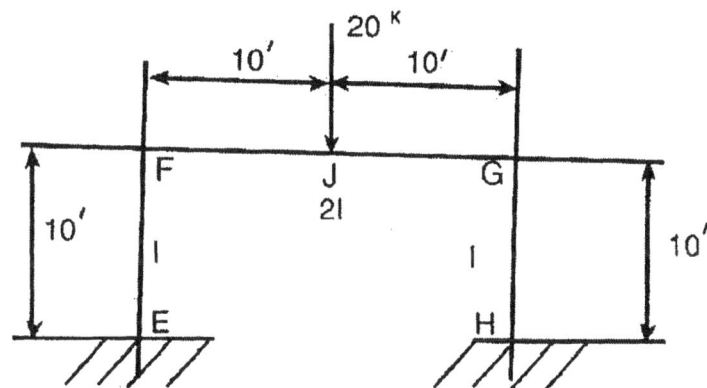

1. The vertical reaction at E is, in kips, MOST NEARLY   1.____
   A. 5   B. 7.5   C. 10   D. 12.5

2. The magnitude of the moment at F on beam FG is, in foot-kips, MOST NEARLY   2.____
   A. 25   B. 27.5   C. 30   D. 35

3. The magnitude of the moment at E on beam EF is, in foot-kips, MOST NEARLY   3.____
   A. 12.5   B. 13.8   C. 15   D. 17.5

4. The horizontal reaction at E is, in kips, MOST NEARLY   4.____
   A. 2.6   B. 3.0   C. 3.4   D. 3.8

5. The moment, in foot-kips, at J is   5.____
   A. 65   B. 70   C. 75   D. 80

31

Questions 6-11.

DIRECTIONS: Questions 6 through 11, inclusive, are to be answered on the basis of the following truss.

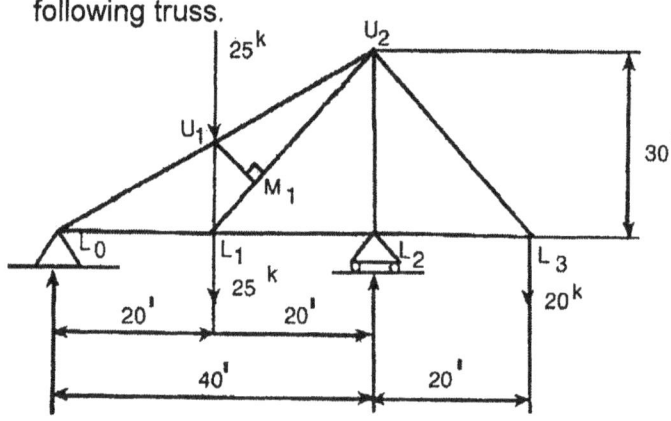

6. The length of the member U_1-M_1 is MOST NEARLY
   A. 8.3 ft.   B. 8.6 ft.   C. 8.9 ft.   D. 9.2 ft.

   6._____

7. The load in member U_1-M_1 is MOST NEARLY
   A. 0
   B. 15k compression
   C. 20k compression
   D. 25k compression

   7._____

8. The load in member U_2-L_2 is MOST NEARLY _____ compression.
   A. 55^k B. 50^k C. 45^k D. 40^k

   8._____

9. The load in member U_1-L_1 is MOST NEARLY _____ compression.
   A. 10^k B. 15^k C. 20^k D. 25^k

   9._____

10. The load in member L_1-U_2 is MOST NEARLY _____ tension.
    A. 50k   B. 55k   C. 60k   D. 65k

    10._____

11. The load in member U_1-U_2 is MOST NEARLY _____ compression.
    A. 20k   B. 25k   C. 30k   D. 35k

    11._____

12. If the center support of the uniformly loaded beam settles slightly, then the
    A. reaction at F increases
    B. magnitude of the moment at F increases
    C. magnitude of the shear at G decreases
    D. reaction at E increases

    12._____

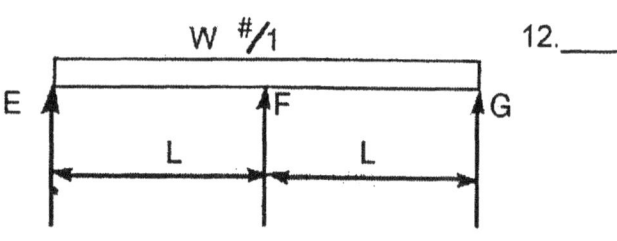

Questions 13-16.

DIRECTIONS: Questions 13 through 16, inclusive, are to be answered on the basis of the truss shown below carrying a uniform moving live load of 2 kips per foot.

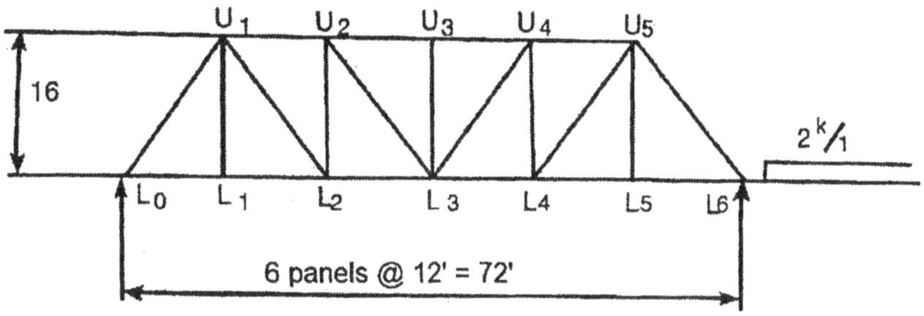

13. The type of truss shown above is known as a _____ truss. 13.____
    A. Pratt B. Howe C. Warren D. Whipple

14. The influence line diagram for member U_2-L_3 is as shown in 14.____

A.

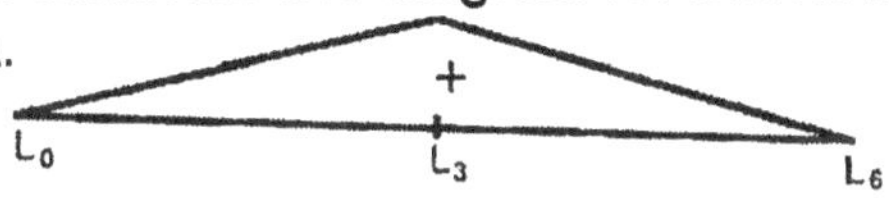

B.

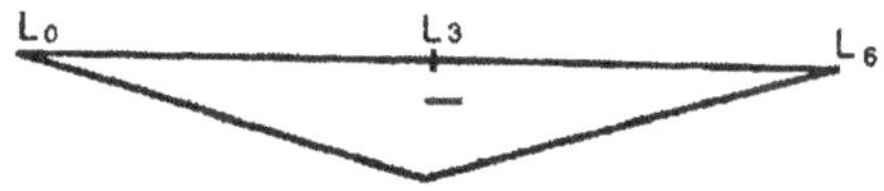

C.

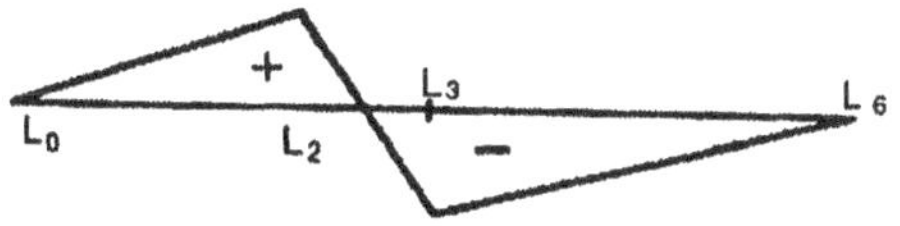

D.

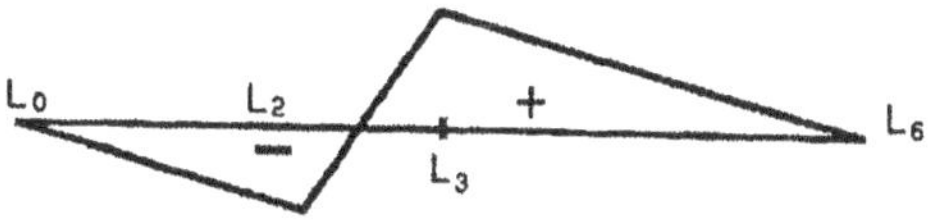

15. The ordinate on the influence line diagram for U_2-L_3 at L_3 is MOST NEARLY 15.____
    A. 3/8 B. ½ C. 5/8 D. ¾

16. The maximum tensile load on U_2-L_3 caused by a $2^{k/1}$ live load coming from the right end of the truss is, in kips, MOST NEARLY 16.____
    A. 21 B. 23 C. 25 D. 27

17. The largest size weld that can be made in one pass is, in inches, 17.____
    A. 3/16 B. ¼ C. 5/16 D. 3/8

18. The maximum allowable shearing stress on fillet welds made with E7018 welding rods is _____ kips/sq.in. 18.____
    A. 18 B. 19 C. 20 D. 21

19. The symbol for field welding is as shown in 19.____

A.

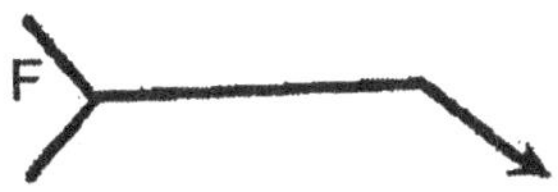

B.

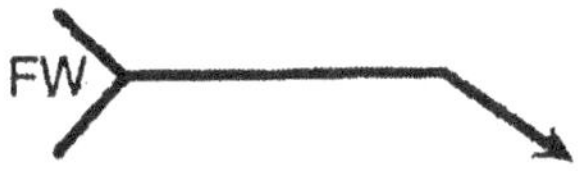

C.

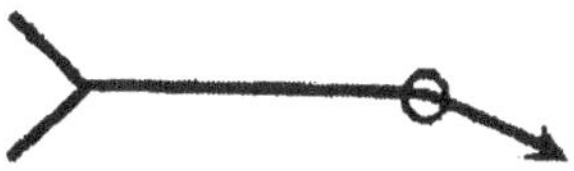

D.

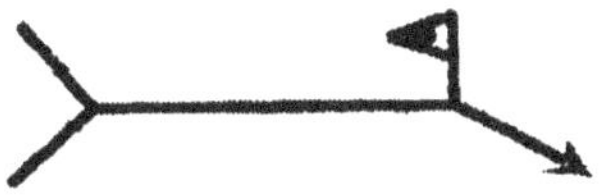

KEY (CORRECT ANSWERS)

1.	C		11.	B
2.	A		12.	D
3.	A		13.	A
4.	D		14.	D
5.	C		15.	C
6.	A		16.	D
7.	A		17.	C
8.	A		18.	D
9.	D		19.	D
10.	C		20.	A

21. C
22. B
23. A
24. C
25. B

TEST 4

DIRECTIONS: Each question or incomplete statement is followed by several suggested answers or completions. Select the one that BEST answers the question or completes the statement. *PRINT THE LETTER OF THE CORRECT ANSWER IN THE SPACE AT THE RIGHT.*

Questions 1-2.

DIRECTIONS: Questions 1 and 2 are to be answered on the basis of the bolted connection supporting a 15k eccentric load shown below.

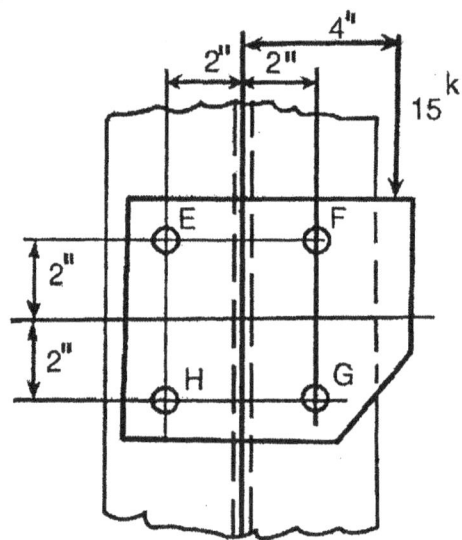

1. The bolts that carry the largest load are
   A. E and F B. F and G C. G and H D. H and E

   1.____

2. The maximum load on a bolt is, in kips, MOST NEARLY
   A. 7.2 B. 7.6 C. 8.0 D. 8.4

   2.____

3. The value of the determinant $\begin{vmatrix} 2 & 1 & 3 \\ 1 & 5 & -6 \\ 1 & 2 & 0 \end{vmatrix}$ is
   A. +3 B. +6 C. +9 D. +12

   3.____

4. $\int_0^{\pi/4} \cos x \sin^2 x \, dx$ is equal to
   A. $\frac{\sqrt{2}}{10}$ B. $\frac{\sqrt{2}}{12}$ C. $\frac{\sqrt{2}}{14}$ D. $\frac{\sqrt{2}}{16}$

   4.____

5. In the xy plane, the distance from point E to the line y = x + 2 is
   A. $\sqrt{2}$
   B. $2\sqrt{2}$
   C. $3\sqrt{3}$
   D. $4\sqrt{2}$

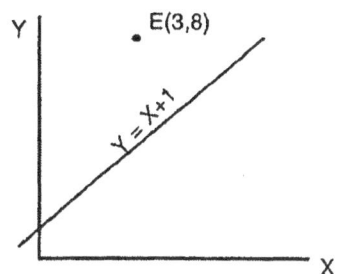

6. The area of the ellipse is $\frac{x^2}{a^2} + \frac{y^2}{b^2} = 1$
   A. $\frac{\pi ab}{4}$
   B. $\frac{\pi ab}{2}$
   C. πab
   D. $\frac{3}{2}\pi ab$

7. Of the following matrix multiplications, the one that cannot be carried out is
   A. $\begin{bmatrix} e & f \\ g & h \end{bmatrix} \begin{bmatrix} j \\ k \end{bmatrix}$
   B. $\begin{bmatrix} e & f \\ g & h \end{bmatrix} [j \ k]$
   C. $[e \ f \ g] \begin{bmatrix} h \\ j \\ k \end{bmatrix}$
   D. $\begin{bmatrix} e \\ f \\ g \end{bmatrix} [h \ j \ k]$

8. Of the following statements relating to matrix operations, the one that is NOT correct is the _____ law of _____ applies to matrices.
   A. associative; addition
   B. associative; multiplication
   C. commutative; addition
   D. commutative; multiplication

9. The volume of revolution formed by rotating the curve y = sin x about the x axis from x = 0 to x = π is
   A. π^2
   B. $\frac{x^2}{2}$
   C. $\frac{x^2}{3}$
   D. $\frac{x^2}{4}$

10. Based on the prismoidal formula, the volume of earth excavated in cubic yards, if one end is 6'x6', and the other end is 12'x12' and the length is 160', is MOST NEARLY
    A. 460
    B. 480
    C. 500
    D. 520

11. The sin(arc tan $\frac{1}{\sqrt{3}}$) is equal to
    A. $\frac{2}{\sqrt{2}}$
    B. $\frac{1}{2}$
    C. $\frac{\sqrt{3}}{2}$
    D. $\frac{\sqrt{3}}{3}$

12. The sum of the interior angles of an octagon is, in degrees, MOST NEARLY
    A. 960
    B. 1020
    C. 1080
    D. 1140

13. The modulus of elasticity of steel in the metric system is _____ x 10^6kPa.
    A. 210
    B. 240
    C. 270
    D. 300

14. If the density of aluminum is 173 #/cu.ft., the density of aluminum in the metric system is, in kg/m³,
    A. 2500
    B. 2590
    C. 2680
    D. 2770

15. One pound per square inch is equal to, in newtons per square meter, 15.____
    A. 5778   B. 6180   C. 6582   D. 6984

16. The moment at E on the beam shown at the right is, in foot-kips, MOST NEARLY   16.____
    A. 28
    B. 32
    C. 36
    D. 40

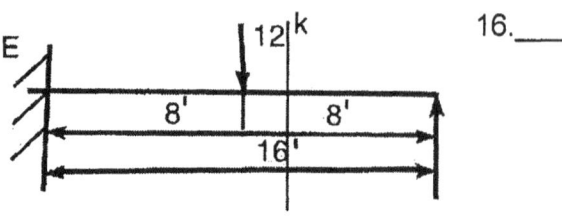

Questions 17-19.

DIRECTIONS: Questions 17 through 19 are to be answered on the basis of the simply supported beam shown below.

A wood beam 8x20# carries a uniform load (including the weight of the wood beam) of 800 #/1 including a 800# load 4 feet from the left end of a simply supported beam on a span of 16 feet as shown below.

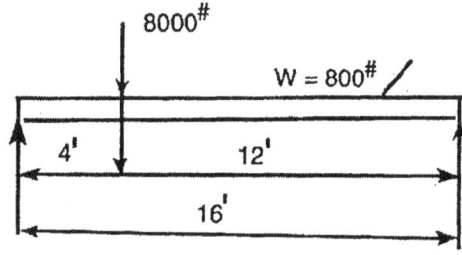 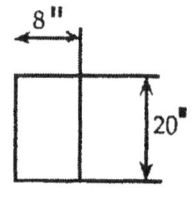

17. The of 0 shear is at a distance from the left support, in feet, MOST NEARLY   17.____
    A. 4.0   B. 4.5   C. 5.0   D. 5.5

18. The maximum bending stress is, in pounds per square inch, MOST NEARLY   18.____
    A. 900   B. 930   C. 960   D. 990

19. The maximum shearing stress is, in pounds per square inch, MOST NEARLY   19.____
    A. 116   B. 130   C. 146   D. 162

20. The cross-section area of a w 12x22 steel beam is, in square inches, MOST NEARLY   20.____
    A. 6.17   B. 6.47   C. 6.77   D. 7.07

21. A welding electrode is specified as E7018.   21.____
    Of the following statements relating to the electrode, the one that is CORRECT is the
    A. 70 relates to the tensile strength of the weld in kips per square inch
    B. 70 is the Charpy V-Notch Test requirement that must be met
    C. 1 represents the coating characteristic
    D. 8 represents the position code

22. In tall steel frame buildings, the columns are usually erected in lengths of _____ story(ies).
    A. 1   B. 2   C. 3   D. 4

23. In a L6x4x½ , the distance from the back of the 4 inch leg to the center of gravity of the angle is, in inches, MOST NEARLY
    A. 1.60   B. 1.80   C. 2.00   D. 2.20

24. In the Atterberg Test for soil, a standard brass cup is partly filled with wet soil. A groove of standard dimension is cut in the soil. The cup is lifted and dropped one centimeter 25 times.
    The purpose of this test is to determine the _____ of the soil.
    A. plastic limit   B. plastic index
    C. shrinkage limit   D. liquid limit

25. In the Atterberg Test for soil, the water content at which a $1/8$ inch diameter thread of soil begins to crumble when rolled under the palm of the hand is known as the _____ of the soil.
    A. plastic limit   B. plastic index
    C. shrinkage limit   D. liquid limit

KEY (CORRECT ANSWERS)

1.	B	11.	B
2.	D	12.	C
3.	C	13.	A
4.	B	14.	D
5.	B	15.	D
6.	C	16.	C
7.	B	17.	D
8.	D	18.	D
9.	B	19.	A
10.	C	20.	B

21. A
22. B
23. C
24. D
25. A

EXAMINATION SECTION
TEST 1

DIRECTIONS: Each question or incomplete statement is followed by several suggested answers or completions. Select the one that BEST answers the question or completes the statement. *PRINT THE LETTER OF THE CORRECT ANSWER IN THE SPACE AT THE RIGHT.*

1. In pipe laying, the required width of trench in sand is less than that in clay because 1.____

   A. of the dilatancy of the sand
   B. the sand gives the pipe a more uniform support
   C. sand backfill puts less load upon the pipe
   D. of backfilling requirements
   E. it is easier to enlarge the trench for bell holes in sand

2. A short post, 12 inches in diameter, is subjected to 75K applied 1" from the center. The maximum stress in the post, in lbs./sq.in., is MOST NEARLY 2.____

   A. 290   B. 995   C. 1,100   D. 1,260   E. 1,340

3. Of the following, the geological feature which will have the LEAST effect on a foundation is 3.____

   A. stratification   B. foliation or cleavage
   C. striation   D. dip and strike
   E. faults

4. In tall steel frame buildings, the columns are usually erected in lengths of 4.____

   A. 16 feet   B. 20 feet
   C. one story   D. two stories
   E. three stories

5. The P.C. of a 7° curve is at Sta. 16+25.0. The deflection angle to Sta. 17+00 is 5.____

   A. 4° 29'   B. 3° 18'   C. 2° 38'   D. 1° 97'   E. 0° 42'

6. Reverse curves on highways are customarily separated by tangents. Of the following, the BEST reason for this separation is 6.____

   A. to increase sight-distance
   B. to increase the radii of the curves
   C. to improve the appearance of the highway
   D. to avoid sudden changes in curvature
   E. concerned with superelevation

7. The modulus of rupture of a wooden beam is 7.____

   A. greater than the ultimate strength in tension
   B. less than the ultimate strength in tension
   C. a function of the shearing strength if the beam is long
   D. less than the ultimate strength in compression
   E. independent of the cross-section of the beam

8. Plain sedimentation is usually preferred to chemical precipitation in sewage treatment because

   A. disposition of the sludge resulting from chemical precipitation is difficult
   B. it removes a greater percentage of total suspended matter
   C. it removes a greater percentage of organic matter
   D. chemical precipitation always increases the pH concentration
   E. the resulting sludge is not putrescible

9. The strength of clay sewer pipe is NOT usually determined by a(n) _____ test.

   A. two-edge bearing B. three-edge bearing
   C. sand bearing D. *knife-edge*
   E. Izod or impact

10. The maximum moment that three moving loads of 6, 8, and 10 kips, from left to right, respectively, spaced 6 feet apart, can cause on a span of 30 feet is, in K feet,

    A. 110 B. 120.4 C. G. 152.6 D. 132.2 E. 95.1

11. In stream flow, a curve of rate of discharge versus gage height is known as a

    A. rating curve B. mass diagram
    C. Rippl diagram D. flood curve
    E. calibration curve

12. An inverted syphon carries a canal from one side of a valley at Elev. 100 to the other at Elev. 95. Assuming the coefficient of pipe friction is independent of diameter, the required diameter of pipe varies as

    A. $Q^{9/10}$ B. $Q^{4/5}$ C. $Q^{3/5}$ D. $Q^{2/5}$ E. $Q^{1/5}$

13. Two pipe lines carrying water are at the same elevation. Each is connected to a Bourdon Gage, the center of which is 4 feet vertically above the pipe center.
    If one gage registers 10 feet and the other minus 2 feet, the difference in pressure between the two pipes, in pounds per square inch, is about

    A. 6.9 B. 6.7 C. 5.9 D. 4.7 E. 3.9

14. The reason wooden beams bearing on brick walls are cut at the end with a mitre is

    A. a precaution in the event of fire
    B. so the inspector can be sure the beam is well seated
    C. to expose a fresh surface so that faulty wood may be detected
    D. that beams so cut may be placed more easily
    E. to make fire-stopping easier

15. Of the following conditions, shearing stress in the web of rolled steel beams is MOST likely to influence the choice of section when

    A. headroom requires the use of a section shallower than the most economical section
    B. the span is long and carries several uniformly spaced concentrated loads
    C. the deflection is small
    D. the span is long and carries two heavy concentrated loads, one near each support
    E. the span is long and uniformly loaded

16. The gridiron system of water distribution is 16.____

   A. preferable to the branching system with regard to fire protection
   B. only used in the largest cities
   C. less advantageous than the branching system because it requires a superimposed high pressure system
   D. being replaced by the branching system
   E. impractical in developments with many curved streets

17. An advantage of reinforced concrete beam and girder construction, as compared to flat slab construction, is 17.____

   A. greater fire resistance
   B. cheaper form work
   C. sprinkler layout is easier
   D. ventilation of rooms is easier
   E. none of the above

18. Activated sludge is sludge that 18.____

   A. is mixed mechanically
   B. has been *seeded*
   C. is stirred by air currents which give it a spiral motion
   D. is agitated in any one of several ways
   E. has been removed from a drying bed

19. In water purification, *aeration* is used to remove 19.____

   A. turbidity   B. dissolved oxygen
   C. sediment   D. organic material
   E. objectionable gases

20. The maximum unit stress to which a material may be subjected without suffering permanent deformation is known as the 20.____

   A. elastic limit   B. yield strength
   C. proportional limit   D. yield point
   E. commercial elastic limit

21. The distance in inches from the back of the short leg to the center of gravity of a 5" x 4" x 1/2" steel angle is APPROXIMATELY 21.____

   A. 0.80   B. 1.15   C. 1.40   D. 1.55   E. 1.60

22. A symmetrical triangular roof truss of four panels at 10 feet having a span of 40 feet between end supports and a rise of 10 feet carries a vertical load at the top center of 20,000 pounds. 22.____
The stress in the upper chord of the end panel, in pounds, is APPROXIMATELY

   A. 15,500   B. 19,500   C. 22,500   D. 26,500   E. 28,500

23. A short concrete column with an effective cross-section 30 inches square has two percent vertical steel reinforcing with proper tie. 23.____
Assuming f_c = 500 pounds per square inch, n = 15, the live load that can safely be carried by this column is
MOST NEARLY _____ pounds.

   A. 550,000   B. 575,000   C. 650,000   D. 675,000   E. 700,000

4 (#1)

24. A welded cylindrical horizontal steel tank 36 inches in diameter is subjected to an internal pressure caused by 72-foot head of water. The ends of the tank are capped with hemispherical heads extending outward.
    If the allowable tensile strength of the steel be taken as 18,000 lbs. per sq. in., the theoretical thickness of the heads should be, in inches,

    A. 0.735   B. 0.015   C. 0.475   D. 0.625   E. 0.375

25. Water flows from reservoir A, elev. 178, to reservoir B, elev. 106, through 3220 feet of 6" pipe; f = .02.
    The velocity in the pipe, in ft./sec., is MOST NEARLY

    A. 1   B. 2   C. 3.5   D. 4.5   E. 6

26. Water is flowing through an open channel of triangular cross-section. The side slopes of the channel are 1:1. The water is 8 feet deep.
    The hydraulic radius is

    A. 7.65   B. 6.40   C. 4.37   D. 3.59   E. 2.82

27. The building code of the large city specifies that bearing piles of wood shall not be spaced closer center to center, in inches, than

    A. 20   B. 24   C. 28   D. 32   E. 36

28. The four sides of a rectangular pier have a uniform batter of 2 inches per foot.
    If the top of the pier is 4 feet by 10 feet and the pier is 12 feet high, the volume, to the NEAREST cubic foot, is

    A. 668   B. 880   C. 992   D. 745   E. 858

29. To lay out a line 170.00 feet long with a 100-foot tape which is actually 100.03 feet long, the taped distance should be

    A. 169.03   B. 169.95   C. 170.45   D. 170.50   E. 170.65

30. Of the following, the LEAST satisfactory method of preventing electrolysis in underground pipe lines near street railways is

    A. applying an insulating coat to the pipe
    B. using track joint bonds
    C. using track joint bonds and cross bonds
    D. using insulating joints on the pipe
    E. providing drains for the road bed

31. A uniformly loaded beam is continuous over four uniformly spaced supports, A, B, C, and D, reading from left to right.
    If the support B settles slightly, the

    A. reaction at D decreases   B. reaction at C decreases
    C. moment at C decreases   D. moment at B increases
    E. reaction at A decreases

32. A flanged shaft coupling uses four 1-inch bolts equispaced on a circle 6 inches in radius. When the shaft is transmitting 300 horsepower at 200 r.p.m., the stress in the bolts, in pounds per square inch, is MOST NEARLY

    A. 5000   B. 4500   C. 4000   D. 3500   E. 3000

33. A simple beam on a 16 foot span carries a concentrated load of 5000 pounds at the mid-point.
    If E is 1,600,000 pounds per square inch and I is 1728 inches fourth, the center deflection, in inches, is MOST NEARLY

    A. 0.27   B. 0.39   C. 0.47   D. 0.59   E. 0.67

34. The tensile efficiency of a riveted butt joint with adequate straps is a function of

    A. rivet diameter and plate width
    B. rivet diameter and plate thickness
    C. rivet diameter, plate width, and plate thickness
    D. plate width and thickness
    E. rivet value in double shear and in bearing

35. A 24-inch beam is made up of two 12-inch steel I-beams, the flanges in contact being riveted.
    If the moment of inertia of a single 12-inch beam is 300 inches fourth and the cross-sectional area 15 square inches, the moment of inertia of the 24-inch beam is, in inches fourth, MOST NEARLY

    A. 2390   B. 1680   C. 1540   D. 920   E. 580

36. A distance taped on a 3 percent slope is 231.24 feet. The length, in feet, of the horizontal projection is

    A. 231.14   B. 231.07   C. 231.00   D. 230.93   E. 230.86

37. In running a closed level circuit, 50 set-ups were made. If each of the rod readings varied accidentally by plus or minus 0.003 feet from its correct value, the probable error of closure of the circuit is, in feet,

    A. 0.405   B. 0.325   C. 0.030   D. 0.015   E. 0.005

38. The dry weight of a cubic foot of sand is 104 pounds. The specific gravity of the sand grains is 2.60.
    The submerged weight of a cubic foot of this sand in fresh water is, in pounds,

    A. 56   B. 60   C. 64   D. 68   E. 72

39. A street 40 feet wide with a parabolic cross-section has a crown of 6 inches at the center. The elevation of a point on the street surface 4 feet from the gutter is below the crown a distance, in inches, of

    A. 1.29   B. 2.73   C. 3.84   D. 4.51   E. 5.19

40. Line AB is extended to C with the transit set at A, a single, careful sight being taken. Subsequently, the transit is set at B, and C checked by a *double reverse.* All three points are at the same elevation.
If C fails to check the average of the *double reverse,* the transit is not in adjustment in that

   A. the horizontal axis is not perpendicular to the vertical axis
   B. the line of sight is not perpendicular to the horizontal axis
   C. either *a* or *b* or both may be the cause
   D. the axis of the objective slide does not coincide with the optical axis
   E. the line of sight is not parallel to the long bubble

41. The BEST material to use for a hydraulic-fill dam is a well-graded mixture ranging from

   A. gravel to fine silt
   B. sand to clay
   C. coarse sand to silt
   D. gravel to fine sand
   E. chips to ash

42. A round steel bar, one inch in diameter, is embedded 40 inches in concrete.
The unit tensile stress in the bar which will develop a bond stress of 100 pounds per square inch is, in pounds per square inch, about

   A. 19,000   B. 17,000   C. 16,000   D. 15,000   E. 13,000

43. The MOST important advantage of the Invar tape over the ordinary steel tape is it(s)

   A. will not rust
   B. high modulus of elasticity
   C. low coefficient of thermal expansion
   D. greater strength
   E. cheapness

44. Two clean steel pipes, one 12 inches in diameter, the other 6 inches in diameter, run from one reservoir to another in parallel.
If the slope of the hydraulic gradient is the same for the two pipes, the ratio of the discharge of the larger pipe to that of the smaller is about

   A. 5.6   B. 4.7   C. 3.9   D. 2.3   E. 1.1

45. The use of steel pipe to convey water is desirable because it

   A. never requires an inside coating
   B. can be fabricated by unskilled labor
   C. is not subject to electrolysis
   D. can carry large external loads
   E. does not have to be caulked

46. Reinforcing steel is usually shaped on the job

   A. by heating in a forge
   B. by cutting and welding
   C. by hand bending
   D. never
   E. on a bar-bending table

47. *Bulking* of sand

    A. is a maximum with a water content of about 6%
    B. is of no importance in concrete proportioning
    C. varies directly as the moisture content
    D. is greater for a coarse sand than a fine sand
    E. does not occur unless the sand contains over one-half gallon of water per cubic foot

48. The cinders used in *cinder concrete* should be

    A. thoroughly wetted down at least 24 hours before mixing
    B. thoroughly dry before mixing
    C. fine and powdery
    D. at least 50 percent uncombined carbon
    E. at least 50 percent combined carbon

49. Bank-run gravel ordinarily

    A. contains no sand
    B. contains too much sand to make a well-proportioned aggregate for concrete
    C. makes a well-proportioned aggregate for concrete
    D. contains too little sand to make a well-proportioned aggregate for concrete
    E. makes a good binder for macadam roads

50. The practical limit on the depth below water level to which the pneumatic caisson process may be carried is, in feet,

    A. 75   B. 85   C. 95   D. 110   E. 125

KEY (CORRECT ANSWERS)

1. D	11. A	21. D	31. A	41. B
2. C	12. D	22. C	32. A	42. C
3. C	13. A	23. B	33. A	43. C
4. D	14. A	24. B	34. A	44. A
5. C	15. D	25. E	35. B	45. E
6. E	16. A	26. E	36. A	46. E
7. A	17. E	27. B	37. C	47. A
8. A	18. B	28. B	38. C	48. A
9. E	19. E	29. B	39. C	49. B
10. D	20. A	30. A	40. D	50. D

TEST 2

DIRECTIONS: Each question or incomplete statement is followed by several suggested answers or completions. Select the one that BEST answers the question or completes the statement. *PRINT THE LETTER OF THE CORRECT ANSWER IN THE SPACE AT THE RIGHT.*

1. In earthwork, if two stations on a mass diagram have equal ordinates of like sign   1.___

    A. between the two stations, the volume of cut equals the volume of fill
    B. elevation of surface at the two stations is the same
    C. depth of cut or fill at the two stations is the same
    D. the distance between two stations equals the limit of economical haul

2. In the design of a reinforced concrete footing, which carries a reinforced concrete column, the distance from the face of the column to the critical section for shear is, in inches,   2.___

    A. kd   B. jd   C. d   D. zero

3. A major city building code permits reduction in the design live load of columns below the top floor as computed on the basis of design floor load because   3.___

    A. loads on lower floors offset moments created by loads on upper floors
    B. side sway is less when all floors are fully loaded
    C. lower columns are better braced
    D. it is unreasonable to expect all floors to be fully loaded at the same time

4. The term S2S means _____ two sides.   4.___

    A. shellac   B. sandpaper
    C. surfaced   D. split

5. The term *drop panel* is commonly used in   5.___

    A. plastering walls   B. plywood forms
    C. prefabricated housing D. flat slab construction

6. In controlled concrete, the water-cement ratio is selected on the basis of   6.___

    A. consistency desired   B. proportion of aggregates
    C. type of aggregates   D. strength desired

7. A surcharge is usually MOST closely associated with   7.___

    A. highway superelevation   B. very long piles
    C. allowable fluid pressure D. retaining walls

8. Steam at 300 lb./sq.in. flows through a 1 ft. diameter pipe. The pipe walls are 1 in. thick. The unit circumferential stress is, in pounds per square inch,   8.___

    A. 900   B. 1800   C. 3200   D. 4800

9. On a topographic map, the symbol shown at the right represents   9.___
    A. tidal flat
    B. cultivated land
    C. orchard
    D. salt marsh

10. A square steel plate, 8 ft. on a side, is submerged in water with the top edge parallel to the water surface and 10 ft. below the surface.
If the plate makes an angle of 30 with the water surface, the total pressure on the plate is, in pounds,

   A. 2688   B. 8649   C. 31,560   D. 47,900

   10.____

11. The stress in a steel bar 8 feet long, cross-sectional area 4 sq.in., rigidly set in a wall at both ends, due to a temperature rise of 30° F is, in pounds per square inch, ($E = 30 \times 10^6$ lb./sq.in.; coefficient of expansion = 645×10^{-8})

   A. 628   B. 2775   C. 5800   D. 12,235

   11.____

12. The maximum unit stress up to which a material may be stressed without suffering permanent deformation when the stress is removed is called

   A. proportional limit   B. yield point
   C. elastic limit   D. ultimate stress

   12.____

13. The elongation of a steel bar, 100 feet long, cross-sectional area 1 sq.in., supported at one end and hanging vertically, due to its own weight is, in inches,
(Steel weighs 490 lb./cu.ft.; $E = 30 \times 10^6$ lb./sq.in.)

   A. .0019   B. .0068   C. .0077   D. .1586

   13.____

14. Lehoann's solution is used to determine

   A. orientation of a plane table
   B. longitude of station
   C. elevation of B.M. by method of least squares
   D. distances in a triangulation net

   14.____

15. In laying out a circular curve, the formula $R \text{ vers } \frac{1}{2} I$ is used to determine the

   A. middle ordinate   B. tangent distance
   C. long chord   D. external distance

   15.____

16. The results of a survey of a closed traverse are as follows:

Line	Lat.	Dep.
AB	100.62	272.21
BC	153.27	422.16
CD	-322.14	19.23
DA	68.33	-713.50

   The magnitude of the linear error of closure is, in feet,
   A. .04   B. .07   C. .13   D. .15

   16.____

17. The notes for a three level section for a 20 feet wide roadway are

   $\frac{c7.5}{15}$ $\frac{c9}{0}$ $\frac{c12}{18}$

   The cross-sectional area of cut is, in square feet,
   A. 198   B. 246   C. 327   D. 415

   17.____

18. To determine the elevation of a point on the face of a building, a level was set up, a sight of 1.487 taken with a rod on the cap bolt of a hydrant, Elev. 39.470, and another sight taken on a tape with its zero end at the point (the tape stretching downward from the point).
    If the reading on the tape was 1.212, the elevation of the point is

    A. 42.169   B. 41.353   C. 40.457   D. 39.899

19. In taping, an accidental error may result from

    A. the tapeman unintentionally making a mistake
    B. the temperature being greater than that at which tape was standardized
    C. causes beyond control of the tapeman
    D. assuming slope distances to be horizontal distances

20. The maximum shearing stress in a wood joist 3 in. by 10 in., actual dimensions, simply supported at its ends on a 14 feet span, and sustaining a uniform load, including its own weight of 150 lb./ft. over the entire length is, in pounds per square inch,

    A. 39   B. 52   C. 68   D. 126

21. If the moment of inertia of a section is 1500 in. 4, and its area is 12 sq.in., the radius of gyration of the section is, in inches, APPROXIMATELY

    A. 11   B. 27   C. 49   D. 101

22. Of the following types of wall, which one is LEAST like the others in function? _____ wall.

    A. Curtain   B. Retaining   C. Spandrel   D. Wing

23. The bending moment at the ends of a beam rigidly supported at both ends and carrying a uniform load of w #/ft. throughout its entire length 1 ft. is, in ft.lbs.,

    A. $\dfrac{wl^2}{8}$ B. $\dfrac{wl}{10}$ C. $\dfrac{wl^2}{10}$ D. $\dfrac{wl^2}{12}$

24. The hydraulic radius of a rectangular canal 4 feet wide is 1.20.
    The depth of flow, in feet, is

    A. 1.6   B. 2.1   C. 2.6   D. 3.0

25. The dynamic pressure into which the kinetic energy of water is transformed when the valve at the outlet of a pipe is suddenly closed is called

    A. velocity head   B. static head
    C. water hammer   D. hydraulic gradient

26. The length of a 3/8" fillet weld required to resist a shear of 12,000 lbs., if the allowable shearing stress is 13,000 lb./sq.in., is, in inches,

    A. 1.97   B. 2.31   C. 2.77   D. 3.48

27. Bridge trusses are built with a slight camber in order to

    A. make erection easier
    B. avoid sag under load
    C. eliminate secondary stresses
    D. reduce tension in lower chord

28. The formula for determining the value of *n* in concrete design, as given by the A.C.I. and a major city building code is

    A. $\dfrac{3000}{f'c}$ B. $\dfrac{fs}{f'c}$ C. $\dfrac{fs}{fc}$ D. $\dfrac{Es}{fc \times 10^3}$

29. In reinforced concrete design with fs = 18,000 lb./sq.in., fc = 1000 lb./sq.in. and n = 12, the value of k is

    A. .389   B. .396   C. .400   D. .420

30. Water flows through a 2" ⌀ orifice in the side of a tank under a head of 20 ft. If Cd = .60, the quantity of discharge is, in cfs,

    A. .47   B. .91   C. 1.27   D. 239.4

31. Water discharges through a turbine at the rate of 60,000 cfm under a head of 100 ft. If the efficiency of the turbine is 70%, the horsepower developed by the turbine is

    A. 646   B. 7,950   C. 21,300   D. 44,440

32. Stirrups are used in concrete construction to

    A. support reinforcing rods
    B. reinforce concrete for the diagonal tension component of shear
    C. hold forms together
    D. prevent cracking of concrete due to changes of temperature

33. In the design of a steel member in tension, rivet holes must be deducted to obtain the net section.
    This is not done when the member is in compression because

    A. rivet holes are smaller
    B. formulae for design of compression members reduce allowable stress
    C. rivets can be placed more efficiently
    D. rivets are assumed to fill the holes

34. In a specific gravity determination, the weight of a flask full of water is 390.0 grams. The weight of the same flask filled with water and 96.2 grams of sand is 450.0 grams. The specific gravity of the sand is

    A. 2.58   B. 2.66   C. 2.74   D. 2.82

35. A soil has a void ratio of 0.80 and a specific gravity of solids of 2.67.
    The total weight (including the water) of a saturated cubic foot of this soil is, in pounds,

    A. 173.4   B. 120.4   C. 111.1   D. 72.7

36. The loss in head per 1,000 feet in a 12-inch water pipe is 9 feet, and the friction factor, f, is 0.0161.
    The velocity of flow in the pipe is, in feet per second,

    A. 6.0   B. 8.1   C. 13.9   D. 18.3

Questions 37-40.

DIRECTIONS: Questions 37 through 40 refer to the truss shown below.

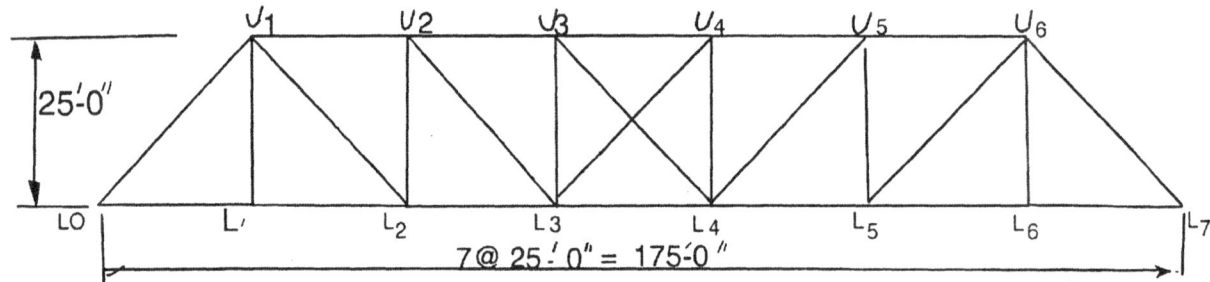

37. If a uniformly distributed live load of 2 kips per foot extends over the entire length of the truss, the live load shear in panel L_2L_3 is, in kips,

    A. 150   B. 100   C. 50   D. 0

38. If the stress in U_2L_2 is -150 kips (compression) and in L_1L_2 +300 kips (tension), the stress in L_2L_3 is, in kips,

    A. +619   B. +450   C. +324   D. +108

39. For a uniformly distributed live load, the maximum tensile stress in member U_2L_3 will occur when the truss is loaded from the

    A. right up to panel point L_3
    B. right up to a point between L_3 and L_2
    C. left up to panel point L_2
    D. left up to a point between L_2 and L_3

40. For a uniformly distributed live load, the maximum tensile stress in member U_2L_2 will occur when the truss is loaded from the left up to

    A. panel point L_3
    B. panel point L_2
    C. a point midway between L_2 and L_3
    D. a point 8'4" from L_2 in panel L_2L_3

KEY (CORRECT ANSWERS)

1.	A	11.	C	21.	A	31.	B
2.	C	12.	C	22.	A	32.	B
3.	D	13.	B	23.	D	33.	D
4.	C	14.	A	24.	D	34.	B
5.	D	15.	A	25.	C	35.	B
6.	D	16.	C	26.	D	36.	A
7.	D	17.	B	27.	B	37.	C
8.	B	18.	A	28.	A	38.	B
9.	D	19.	C	29.	C	39.	B
10.	D	20.	B	30.	A	40.	D

TEST 3

DIRECTIONS: Each question or incomplete statement is followed by several suggested answers or completions. Select the one that BEST answers the question or completes the statement. *PRINT THE LETTER OF THE CORRECT ANSWER IN THE SPACE AT THE RIGHT.*

1. A grit chamber is an enlarged channel through which sewage flows

    A. while being screened
    B. with a velocity of from 0.6 to 2.6 feet per minute
    C. with a velocity reduced to cause heavy solids to be deposited
    D. depositing grit which decomposes in the bottom
    E. in recessed chambers

2. An end post is

    A. a long column
    B. a diagonal compression member
    C. a short column
    D. the end member of a compression chord on a through truss
    E. the outside vertical member of a bent

3. A strut is

    A. a long column
    B. a diagonal compression member
    C. a wide column
    D. the end member of a compression chord on a through truss
    E. the outside vertical member of a bent

4. Of the following items, the one which has NOTHING to do with stadia computations is

    A. Cox computer B. Beaman arc
    C. stadia slide rule D. stadia tables
    E. gradienter

5. In laying up a brick wall, bond refers to the

    A. adhesive property of the mortar
    B. anchors or ties which hold a brick veneer wall to a building
    C. beam anchors
    D. use of bats or half bricks
    E. use of headers and stretchers

6. In a reinforced concrete building of the slab beam and girder type, architectural considerations limit the size of one beam to such an extent that the concrete stress in that beam is excessive.
The MOST practical solution is to

    A. ignore the architectural considerations
    B. use a better quality concrete throughout the building
    C. use a better quality concrete in the beam under consideration
    D. increase the required tension steel
    E. provide compression steel

7. A reinforced concrete beam 10" wide x 12" effective depth, on a simple span of 12'0", is reinforced in tension only with three 1/2" square rods.
   If the allowable steel and concrete stresses are 18,000 and 600 p.s.i., respectively, and K is 1/3, the maximum uniform load that the beam can carry (including its own weight) is, in pounds per foot,

   A. 592   B. 623   C. 667   D. 689   E. 714

8. A statically indeterminate structure

   A. is one to which the equations of static equilibrium do not apply
   B. is statically indeterminate because of secondary stresses
   C. requires more material than an equivalent statically determinate structure because of the uncertainty of the exact values of the stresses in the former
   D. is statically indeterminate because of rigid joints
   E. requires at least one equation in addition to those of static equilibrium, for a solution

9. A masonry wall with a rectangular cross-section is 14 feet high.
   If water stands behind the wall two feet below its top and if the masonry weighs 150 pounds per cubic foot, the required width of the wall to just prevent overturning is, in feet,

   A. 4.14   B. 4.54   C. 5.24   D. 5.84   E. 6.04

10. If the hydraulic radius of a stream is close to unity, the cross-section of the stream is

    A. semi-circular   B. square
    C. triangular   D. deep and narrow
    E. wide and shallow

11. In column formulae, allowance for accidental eccentricity

    A. is made in the factor of safety
    B. is a function of length
    C. is not made
    D. depends only on the section of the column
    E. must be estimated by the designer

12. An emergency pipe line connecting two reservoirs consists of 3,000 feet of 16" pipe followed by 6,000 feet of 24" pipe which leads into the lower reservoir.
    The hydraulic grade line for this pipe

    A. does not drop continuously in the direction of flow
    B. drops continuously in the direction of flow
    C. is affected by the ground profile
    D. is affected by the pipe profile
    E. never rises in the direction of flow

13. The use of several pipes rather than one pipe in an inverted syphon carrying a sewer under a subway is considered good practice because

    A. it helps prevent deposition in the syphon
    B. it reduces the headroom required
    C. several small pipes are cheaper than one big one
    D. the resultant head loss is smaller
    E. it reduces the velocity of flow

14. If the objective lens of a transit telescope is focused to give an observer the clearest possible view of an object,

    A. no parallax can exist
    B. the proper way to eliminate parallax would involve refocusing of both objective and eyepiece
    C. parallax should be ignored
    D. any error due to parallax can be eliminated by a direct and a reversed sight
    E. nothing can be done to eliminate any parallax that may exist

15. The ground rod at Sta. 18+00 is 6.2. If the grade rod is 8.8,

    A. the fill is 3.7
    B. the cut is 14.8
    C. the fill is 15.0
    D. there is no way of telling whether there is cut or fill of 14.8
    E. there is no way of telling whether there is cut or fill of 3.7

16. In a circular curve of radius R and central angle I, the distance $R\left(\dfrac{1}{\cos\frac{1}{2}} - 1\right)$ is used to locate the

    A. point of curvature
    B. point of intersection or vertex
    C. center of the curve from the vertex
    D. midpoint of the chord of the circular curve
    E. midpoint of the long chord

17. A line 442.25 feet long is to be laid out with a 100-foot steel tape which is 100.07 feet long.
    The taped length which should be laid out in the field is

    A. 441.94   B. 441.99   C. 442.04   D. 442.09   E. 442.14

18. Water flows from reservoir A, Elev. 100, to reservoir B through 16,100 feet of 12-inch pipe.
    If the friction factor, f, is 0.02 and the flow 3.14 cubic feet per second, the elevation of the water surface in reservoir B is MOST NEARLY

    A. 32   B. 28   C. 24   D. 20   E. 16

19. The area bounded by the X-axis, the ordinates x = 1 and x = 4, and the curve $y = x^2 - 6x - 7$ is

    A. 45   B. 41   C. 37   D. 33   E. 29

20. A tie rod 20'0" long and one inch in diameter, fastened to rigid supports at its ends, is under a tension of 10,000 p.s.i. when the temperature is 68° F.
    If the temperature rises to 98° F, the tension in the rod will be MOST NEARLY, in p.s.i.,

    A. 4140   B. 5960   C. 7235   D. 10,800   E. 13,444

21. A 14 WF 246 section has a cross-sectional area, in square inches, of about

    A. 63.5   B. 72.5   C. 76.5   D. 80.5   E. 84.5

22. A load of lumber consists of 25 pieces 4" x 6" x 15'3". The total F.B.M. is MOST NEARLY

    A. 8160   B. 6640   C. 762   D. 868   E. 2155

23. In concrete work, the slump test

    A. is used to determine time of initial set
    B. may be used as a rough check of the water-cement ratio
    C. could give identical results for two concrete mixes of entirely different water-cement ratios
    D. is used in the field only after the concrete has proper workability
    E. is gradually being replaced by the Vicat apparatus

24. A gusset plate is attached to one flange of an H-section column by four rivets which lie at the corners of a 6" x 8" rectangle with the 6" side horizontal. The plate carries a vertical concentrated load with action line 20 inches to the right of the center of the rivet group. Lettering the rivets a, b, c, and d in clockwise order starting at the upper lefthand corner, the maximum total rivet stress occurs in

    A. a and b   B. b and d   C. b *only*
    D. b and c   E. c and d

25. A steel I-beam with a section modulus of 120 inches cubed is to carry a uniformly-distributed load including its own weight on a simple span of 12'0". The maximum allowable fibre stress is 16,000 p.s.i.
    Of the following loads, in pounds per foot (including the weight of the beam), the largest load the beam can carry is

    A. 767   B. 2890   C. 8800   D. 19,705   E. 24,664

26. A flat plate carrying a tensile load of 24,000 pounds is to be connected to a gusset plate by means of 5/16" fillet welds.
    If the allowable unit shearing stress on welds is 11,300 p.s.i., the total length of weld required, in inches, is MOST NEARLY

    A. 27.4   B. 17.3   C. 9.6   D. 7.7   E. 6.6

27. The latitudes and departures of a closed traverse are as follows:

Line	Latitude	Departure
AB	+1000	0
BC	0	+1000
CA	-998	-998

    The error of closure is MOST NEARLY

    A. 1:1200   B. 1:1000   C. 1:800   D. 1:500   E. 1:300

28. The flanges and web of an H-section 12" wide by 12" deep are each 1" thick.
The moment of inertia of the section about an axis through the center of gravity and parallel to the flanges is, in inches fourth,

   A. 263   B. 387   C. 595   D. 811   E. 929

29. A circular gate 4' in diameter lies in a vertical plane with its top 4' below the water surface.
The total water pressure on one side of the gate, in pounds, is MOST NEARLY

   A. 800   B. 3200   C. 3700   D. 4700   E. 4500

30. Two 3/8" plates under a tension of 50,000 lbs. are lap riveted with 7/8" rivets. Allowable unit values of rivets are 15,000 lbs. p.s.i. for shear and 32,000 lbs. p.s.i. for bearing.
The number of 7/8" rivets required for this joint is

   A. 1   B. 2   C. 3   D. 4   E. 6

31. A Warren-type deck truss with a span of 60' 0" has 3 panels at 20' 0" and is 20' 0" deep. Under a uniform load of one kip per foot per truss, the maximum stress in the compression chord is, in kips,

   A. 40   B. 35   C. 30   D. 20   E. 10

32. The allowable tensile and bond stresses in reinforcing bars for concrete are 16,000 and 100 p.s.i., respectively. The depth of embedment, in inches, required to develop the allowable tensile strength of a 3/4" diameter bar is

   A. 50   B. 30   C. 20   D. 10   E. 5

33. A sedimentation tank is an enlarged channel through which sewage flows

   A. while being screened
   B. with a velocity of from 0.5 to 2.5 feet per minute
   C. with a velocity reduced to cause heavy solids to be deposited
   D. depositing grit which decomposes in the bottom
   E. in recessed chambers

34. A level is set up so that a Philadelphia rod reads 4.00 on B.M.A., elev. 90.00. A tape rod is then set to read 0.00 at B.M.A. and reads 0.84 at point B.
The elevation of point B is

   A. computed from the H.I.   B. 90.84
   C. 90.37   D. 88.74
   E. 87.14

35. A Proctor compaction test is usually MOST closely associated with the use in the field of a

   A. drag line   B. bulldozer
   C. pile driver   D. sheep's-foot roller
   E. post-hole digger

36. The MOST important consideration in the design of a building foundation resting on a deep clay layer is concerned with

   A. minimum settlement
   B. differential settlement
   C. length of construction period
   D. weather conditions during construction
   E. shape of footing

37. The discharge of a stream varies from 0.1 to 10.0 cubic feet per second, with a mean discharge of about 0.3 c.f.s. The BEST type of weir to measure flow in this stream is

   A. suppressed rectangular
   B. contracted rectangular
   C. trapezoidal
   D. submerged
   E. triangular

38. A peg test on a transit has been completed.
   The first step in the actual adjustment based on the result of the test involves movement of

   A. a diagonally-opposite pair of foot screws
   B. the cross-hair ring
   C. the long bubble by means of the bubble-adjusting screw
   D. the telescope about the horizontal axis
   E. the plate bubbles

39. A steel specimen was tested to destruction in a tension test in which no extensometer was used.
   Results which could be reported would include

   A. elastic limit
   B. yield point
   C. modulus of elasticity
   D. proportional limit
   E. initial set

40. Of the five items following, which one bears the LEAST relationship to the other four?

   A. Shore
   B. Needle
   C. Pretest pile
   D. Underpinning
   E. Pile loading test

KEY (CORRECT ANSWERS)

1. C	11. B	21. B	31. D
2. D	12. A	22. C	32. B
3. B	13. A	23. C	33. B
4. E	14. B	24. D	34. B
5. E	15. C	25. C	35. D
6. E	16. C	26. C	36. B
7. A	17. A	27. A	37. E
8. E	18. D	28. D	38. D
9. A	19. A	29. D	39. B
10. E	20. A	30. E	40. E

EXAMINATION SECTION
TEST 1

DIRECTIONS: Each question or incomplete statement is followed by several suggested answers or completions. Select the one that BEST answers the question or completes the statement. *PRINT THE LETTER OF THE CORRECT ANSWER IN THE SPACE AT THE RIGHT.*

1. An unbalanced bid is a bidding device used by the contractor. An example of unbalanced bidding is to put

   A. lower unit prices in all unit price items to submit a low bid
   B. lower prices on lump sum items and higher prices on unit price items
   C. lower unit prices on secondary items and higher unit prices on primary items
   D. higher prices on items built early and lower prices on items built later

   1.____

2. Clearing and grubbing as related to excavation mean cutting trees

   A. so that 1 foot remains above ground
   B. so that 6 inches remains above ground
   C. to ground level
   D. and removing the stumps of the trees

   2.____

3. The size of a bulldozer is measured by its

   A. weight   B. flywheel horsepower
   C. ripping capacity   D. coefficient of traction

   3.____

4. Of the following, an important use of geotextiles is

   A. as a filter in drainage control
   B. to improve the density of soil
   C. to increase the plasticity of soil
   D. to reduce the CBR of soil

   4.____

5. A graphical procedure employing a control chart is sometimes used for statistical control in highway construction. After charts of individual tests are prepared, the upper and lower limits are usually _____ standard deviation(s) from a central value.

   A. one   B. two   C. three   D. four

   5.____

6. On a highway construction job, slope stakes are usually set on both sides of the road at intervals of _____ feet.

   A. 25   B. 50   C. 75   D. 100

   6.____

7. Earth grade stakes are usually set

   A. when the slope stakes are set
   B. at the center line of the road
   C. after final grading is completed
   D. after rough grading operations have been completed

   7.____

8. In a borrow pit, measurements for the volume of earth removed are taken usually at _____ foot intervals.

   A. 25 B. 50 C. 75 D. 100

9. In placing surveying stakes for a culvert, a stake is set at the center line of the culvert. A horizontal line on the stake gives the amount of cut or fill to the _____ of the culvert.

   A. top B. center C. flow line D. subgrade

10. Aeolian soils are soils formed by

    A. glacial action
    B. volcanic action
    C. being carried by water
    D. being carried by wind

11. Specific gravity of soils are in the range of

    A. 2.3 to 2.5
    B. 2.4 to 2.6
    C. 2.5 to 2.7
    D. 2.6 to 2.8

12. Of the following soils, the one that is most highly compressible has a _____ plastic limit and _____ liquid limit.

    A. low; high
    B. low; low
    C. high; low
    D. high; high

13. In the present ASSHTO soil classification systems, soils are classified into groups. The number of basic groups are

    A. 6 B. 7 C. 8 D. 9

14. In the present AASHTO soil classification system, granular materials are primarily in Group(s)

    A. A1 *only*
    B. A1 and A2
    C. A1, A2, and A3
    D. A1, A2, A3, and A4

15. The optimum moisture content of a soil occurs when under a given compactive effort, the soil has a maximum

    A. void ratio
    B. plasticity index
    C. elasticity
    D. density

16. The liquid limit that separates an A4 soil from an A5 soil is

    A. 10 B. 20 C. 30 D. 40

17. As part of the soil classification in a given soil is an abbreviation NP. This is an abbreviation for no

    A. permeability
    B. plasticity
    C. peat or other organic materials
    D. porosity

18. For granular materials, the maximum allowable percent passing a Number 200 sieve is

    A. 20 B. 25 C. 30 D. 35

19.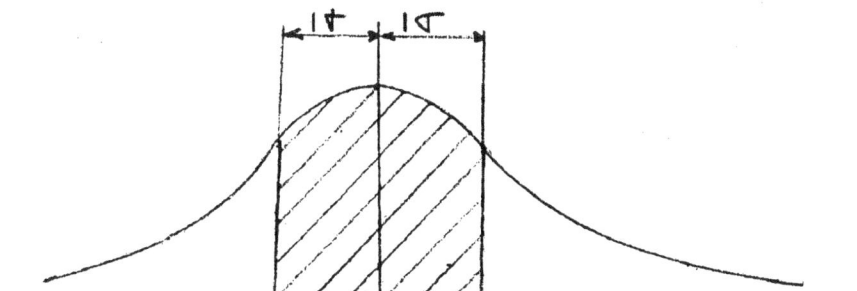

In the normal or Gauss distribution shown above, the shaded area is one standard deviation on either side of the central value covering _____ of the area under the curve.

A. 60%   B. 62%   C. 65%   D. 68%

Questions 20-25.

DIRECTIONS: Questions 20 through 25, inclusive, refer to the diagram below of a vertical curve.

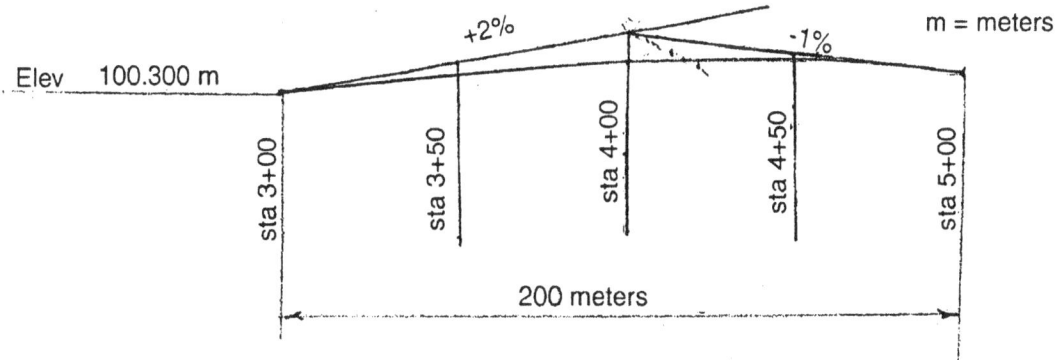

20. The elevation of the curve at Sta4+00 is _____ meters.
    A. 101.250   B. 101.350   C. 101.850   D. 102.150

21. The grade of the curve at Sta4+00 is
    A. +.5%   B. +.75%   C. +1.00%   D. +1.25%

22. The elevation of the curve at Sta3+50 is _____ meters.
    A. 100.992   B. 101.012   C. 101.112   D. 101.212

23. The grade of the curve at Sta3+50 is
    A. 1.75%   B. 1.50%   C. 1.38%   D. 1.25%

24. The station of the high point is
    A. 4+08.333   B. 4+16.667   C. 4+25.000   D. 4+33.333

25. The elevation of the high point is _____ meters.
    A. 101.633   B. 101.750   C. 101.833   D. 101.917

KEY (CORRECT ANSWERS)

1. D
2. D
3. B
4. A
5. C

6. B
7. D
8. A
9. C
10. D

11. D
12. A
13. B
14. C
15. D

16. D
17. B
18. D
19. D
20. B

21. A
22. C
23. D
24. D
25. A

TEST 2

DIRECTIONS: Each question or incomplete statement is followed by several suggested answers or completions. Select the one that BEST answers the question or completes the statement. *PRINT THE LETTER OF THE CORRECT ANSWER IN THE SPACE AT THE RIGHT.*

Questions 1-3.

DIRECTIONS: Questions 1 through 3 refer to the diagram below.

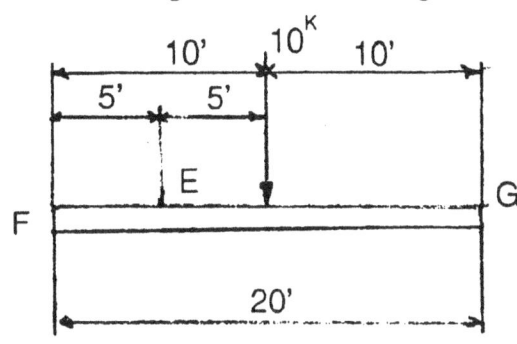

EI is constant

1. The deflection at the center of the beam is

  A. $-\dfrac{1670^{k13}}{EI}$ B. $-\dfrac{2000^{k13}}{EI}$ C. $-\dfrac{2330^{k13}}{EI}$ D. $-\dfrac{2670^{k13}}{EI}$

1.____

2. The slope at F is

  A. $-\dfrac{200^{k12}}{EI}$ B. $-\dfrac{225^{k12}}{EI}$ C. $-\dfrac{250^{k12}}{EI}$ D. $-\dfrac{275^{k12}}{EI}$

2.____

3. The deflection at E is

  A. $-\dfrac{966^{k13}}{EI}$ B. $-\dfrac{1046^{k13}}{EI}$ C. $-\dfrac{1096^{k13}}{EI}$ D. $-\dfrac{1146^{k13}}{EI}$

3.____

Questions 4-7.

DIRECTIONS: Questions 4 through 7, inclusive, refer to the truss below.

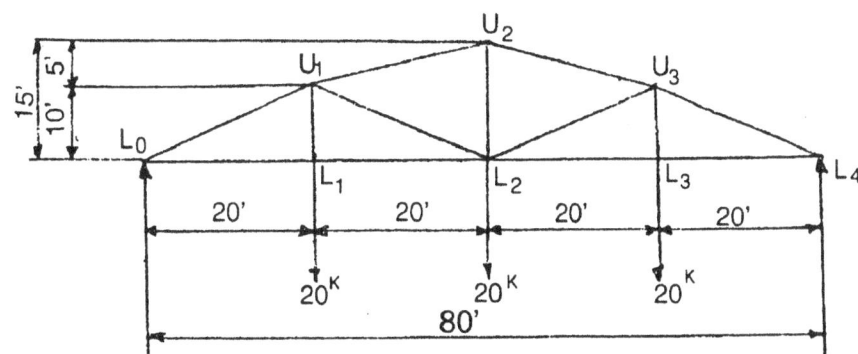

4. The load in member L_1-L_2 is

   A. $+30^k$ B. $+40^k$ C. $+50^k$ D. $+60^k$

5. The load in member U_1-U_2 is

   A. -50.9^k B. -52.9^k C. -54.9^k D. -56.9^k

6. The load in member U_1-L_2 is

   A. -3.4^k B. -5.4^k C. -7.4^k D. -9.4^k

7. The load in member U_2-L_2 is

   A. $+24.6^k$ B. $+26.6^k$ C. $+28.6^k$ D. $+30.6^k$

Questions 8-11.

DIRECTIONS: Questions 8 through 11, inclusive, refer to the diagram below of a beam with fixed ends.

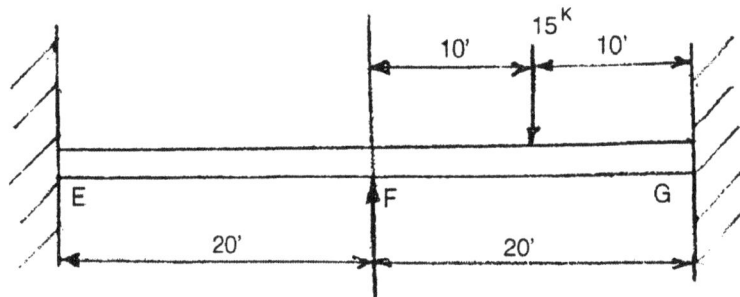

8. The moment in E is

   A. 9.4^{lk} B. 12.6^{lk} C. 14.8^{lk} D. 17.0^{lk}

9. The moment in G is

   A. 37.5^{lk} B. 40.0^{lk} C. 43.0^{lk} D. 46.9^{lk}

10. The moment at F is

    A. 14.4^{lk} B. 18.8^{lk} C. 23.2^{lk} D. 27.6^{lk}

11. The vertical reaction at E is

    A. -0.4^k B. -1.4^k C. -2.4^k D. -3.4^k

12. The former First Lady of the United States who had legislation enacted to plant wild flowers adjacent to federal highways is

    A. Rosalyn Carter
    B. Barbara Bush
    C. Jackie Kennedy
    D. Lady Bird Johnson

13. *Scarification* as used in the specifications means

    A. removing rust from a surface
    B. removing paint from a surface
    C. cleaning equipment
    D. loosening topsoil

14. A proposal by the contractor producing a savings to the department without impairing essential functions and characteristics of the facility is termed a(n)

    A. alternative suggestion
    B. design efficiency proposal
    C. value engineering proposal
    D. force account economy

15. A cubic meter is MOST NEARLY equal to _____ cubic yards.

    A. 1.31   B. 1.33   C. 1.35   D. 1.37

16. One hectare is equal to MOST NEARLY _____ acres.

    A. 2   B. 2.5   C. 3.0   D. 3.5

17. One newton is MOST NEARLY equal to _____ pounds.

    A. .12   B. .17   C. .22   D. .29

18. A metric ton is _____ pounds.

    A. 2200   B. 2400   C. 2600   D. 2800

19. A piezometer is a device that measures

    A. hydraulic pressure   B. soil compaction
    C. soil grain size   D. soil grain strength

20. Portland cement type 2 is _____ cement.

    A. high early strength
    B. low heat
    C. air entraining
    D. moderate sulfate resisting

21. Wire shall have a minimum yield strength of 240 MPa. The MPa is an abbreviation of _____ pascals.

    A. macro   B. micro   C. milli   D. mega

22. 7°C is, in degrees Fahrenheit,

    A. 42.6   B. 44.6   C. 46.6   D. 48.6

23. In a concrete mix, the absolute ratio of the weight of water to the weight of cement is .44. If a bag of cement weighs 94 pounds and there are 7.48 gallons in a cubic foot, the number of gallons of water per bag of cement for this ratio is MOST NEARLY

    A. 5.0   B. 5.5   C. 5.8   D. 6.1

24. The specifications require that when transit mixed concrete is used, approximately 90% of the design water is added followed by mixing the concrete in the drum of the truck. The remainder of the design water may be added

    A. after half the load is emptied
    B. to meet the water cement ratio requirement
    C. if the mix is not uniform
    D. to attain a suitable slump

25. For highways, the minimum median width in a divided highway is _____ feet.

    A. 2   B. 3   C. 4   D. 5

KEY (CORRECT ANSWERS)

1. A
2. C
3. D
4. D
5. C

6. C
7. B
8. A
9. D
10. B

11. B
12. D
13. D
14. C
15. A

16. B
17. C
18. A
19. A
20. D

21. D
22. B
23. A
24. D
25. C

EXAMINATION SECTION
TEST 1

DIRECTIONS: Each question or incomplete statement is followed by several suggested answers or completions. Select the one that BEST answers the question or completes the statement. *PRINT THE LETTER OF THE CORRECT ANSWER IN THE SPACE AT THE RIGHT.*

1. The specifications denote the ultimate strength of concrete at the end of _____ days. 1._____

    A. 7 B. 14 C. 21 D. 28

2. The one of the following that is NOT a purpose of adding an admixture to the concrete mixture is 2._____

    A. set retardation
    B. water reduction
    C. required air content
    D. increase hardness

3. When a highway slab is to be placed by slipform paving, it is essential that the concrete mix have a 3._____

    A. large slump
    B. small slump
    C. high air content
    D. low air content

4. Of the following, the accepted method used to insure that the thickness of a sidewalk slab meets the specified minimum depth is to 4._____

    A. have the contractor certify that it meets the specified required depth
    B. measure the depth of the slab at its edge
    C. take a core boring of the slab
    D. place a test load on a square foot of the slab to insure the slab has an adequate bearing capacity

5. Calcium chloride is sometimes added to a concrete mix as a(n) _____ agent. 5._____

    A. retarding
    B. air entraining
    C. curing
    D. accelerating

6. *Pumping* in a highway concrete slab refers to the 6._____

    A. ejection of water and soil along the edges of a concrete slab
    B. raising of a concrete highway slab due to frost heave
    C. bulging of a concrete slab when high temperature causes excessive expansion of a slab at an expansion joint
    D. raising and falling of a concrete slab caused by a rise in the water table

7. The material used in madjacking consists primarily of _____ sand, cement and water. 7._____

    A. gypsum, coarse
    B. coarse
    C. gypsum, fine
    D. fine

8. A gallon of water weighs _____ pounds per cubic foot. 8._____

    A. 8.00 B. 8.15 C. 8.33 D. 8.45

9. Of the following, the one that would NOT be used as a dust palliative on a road surface would be

   A. calcium sulfate
   B. calcium chloride
   C. sodium chloride
   D. bituminous substances

10. One of the items in highway maintenance is *soil sterilants*. The primary purpose of soil sterilants is to

    A. prevent the spread of mosquitos
    B. prevent the growth of weeds
    C. discourage wild animals from using the road
    D. encourage the growth of wild flowers

Questions 11-16.

DIRECTION: Questions 11 through 16, inclusive, refer to the following chart describing the gradation of a subbase for a highway pavement.

Sieve Size Designation	Percent Passing By Weight
75mm	100
50mm	90-100
6.3mm	30-65
425μmm	5-40
75μmm	0-10

11. The maximum percent that can be retained on the 50mm screen is

    A. 0   B. 5   C. 10   D. 15

12. The maximum percent that can be retained on the 6.3mm screen is

    A. 40   B. 50   C. 60   D. 70

13. The minimum percent that must be retained on the 6.3mm screen is

    A. 20   B. 25   C. 30   D. 60

14. The maximum size of aggregate for the subbase is MOST NEARLY _____ inches.

    A. 2   B. 2 1/2   C. 3   D. 3 1/2

15. μmm is equal to a _____ of a meter.

    A. thousandth
    B. ten-thousandth
    C. hundred thousandth
    D. millionth

16. μ in the metric system is a prefix for

    A. milli   B. micro   C. nano   D. pico

17. The specifications state that sodium chloride shall be packed in moisture-proof bags not containing more than 45 kg each.
    The MAXIMUM weight per bag, in pounds, is

    A. 95   B. 97   C. 99   D. 101

18. In placing corrugated steel pipe with longitudinal seams, the longitudinal seams shall be placed   18.____

    A. at the sides of the pipe
    B. at the top of the pipe
    C. at the bottom of the pipe
    D. wherever it is convenient for the contractor

19. In placing corrugated steel pipe, the circumferential seams with laps shall be placed with   19.____

    A. one lap facing upstream and the next lap facing downstream
    B. laps facing in the downstream direction
    C. laps facing in the upstream direction
    D. laps lap welded to the adjacent pipe

20. Before laying corrugated steel pipe, the specifications require that the contractor shall provide the inspector equipment to measure the gauge of the pipe.
    The equipment referred to is a   20.____

    A. micrometer
    B. steel rule that measures to a 64th of an inch
    C. manometer
    D. caliper

21. The thickness of the galvanized coating on a corrugated steel pipe can be measured with a(n)   21.____

    A. fixed probe magnetic gauge
    B. ultrasonic probe
    C. laser gauge
    D. piezometer

22. Terne plate is steel plate coated with   22.____

    A. zinc   B. lead   C. copper   D. tin

23. The cross-section area of a No. 9 reinforcing steel bar is _____ square inches.   23.____

    A. .60   B. .875   C. 1.00   D. 1.128

24. The weight per foot of a No. 9 reinforcing bar is MOST NEARLY _____ pounds per foot.   24.____

    A. 1.8   B. 2.04   C. 3.4   D. 3.64

25. The diameter of a No. 9 bar is _____ inch(es).   25.____

    A. 0.75   B. 0.875   C. 1   D. 1.125

TEST 2

DIRECTIONS: Each question or incomplete statement is followed by several suggested answers or completions. Select the one that BEST answers the question or completes the statement. *PRINT THE LETTER OF THE CORRECT ANSWER IN THE SPACE AT THE RIGHT.*

1. A reinforcing steel bar is designated Grade 40. The 40 refers to its   1.____

    A. allowable working stress
    B. yield point
    C. elastic limit
    D. ultimate strength

2. The epoxy coating of a reinforcing bar is tested by bending the bar 120 about a mandrel of specified diameter. This test is defined as a(n) _____ test.   2.____

    A. adhesion   B. tensile   C. shear   D. bearing

3. The hourly rate of flow of sewage is not constant but varies between _____ percent of the daily average.   3.____

    A. 90 to 110   B. 70 to 130   C. 50 to 150   D. 30 to 170

4. If the slope of a sewer pipe is .003. The change in elevation in 100 feet is   4.____

    A. 3 1/2"   B. 3 5/8"   C. 3 3/4"   D. 4"

5. The minimum allowable velocities in sanitary sewers is _____ feet per second.   5.____

    A. 1 to 1.5   B. 1.5 to 2   C. 2.0 to 2.5   D. 2.5 to 3.0

6. Catch basins are designed to   6.____

    A. slow down the flow of storm water
    B. filter out organic material from the storm water
    C. clean grit before it enters the storm sewer
    D. catch grit admitted through street inlets and prevent it from entering the storm water drains

7. Before workmen go into a manhole to do repair work, it is necessary to suck out the air from the manhole and replace it with fresh air. The MAIN purpose of replacing the air in the sewer manhole is to remove   7.____

    A. methane gas   B. carbon dioxide
    C. carbon disulfide   D. hydrogen disulfide

8. Sewage consists primarily of fresh water and has less than _____ percent of solid matter.   8.____

    A. 0.1   B. 0.2   C. 0.3   D. 0.4

9. Fresh sewage has only a slight odor, but when stale it becomes septic and has a strong _____ odor.   9.____

    A. vinegary   B. sweetish
    C. benzene   D. hydrogen sulfxde

Questions 10-11.

DIRECTIONS: Questions 10 and 11 refer to the section of an existing concrete sewer.

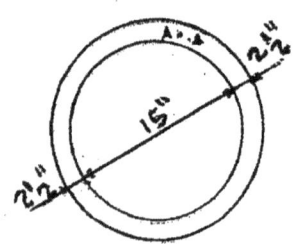

10. If the elevation of the top of the sewer is 24,572 feet, the elevation of the invert of the sewer is ———— feet.

    A. 23.114   B. 23.052   C. 22.965   D. 22.905

11. The cross-section area of the concrete section is sq.in.

    A. 131.5   B. 133.5   C. 135.5   D. 137.5

12. The reason for using wellpoints in the construction of sewers is usually to

    A. prevent the formation of boils
    B. lower the water table
    C. overcome the existence of quicksand
    D. keep the trench dry in the event of a rainstorm

13. Shown at the right is a sewer section with a concrete cradle. The area of the cradle is ____ square feet.
    A. 1.60
    B. 1.66
    C. 1.72
    D. 1.78

14.

The volume of excavation by the prismoidal formula is _____ cubic yards.

    A. 118   B. 123   C. 128   D. 133

15.

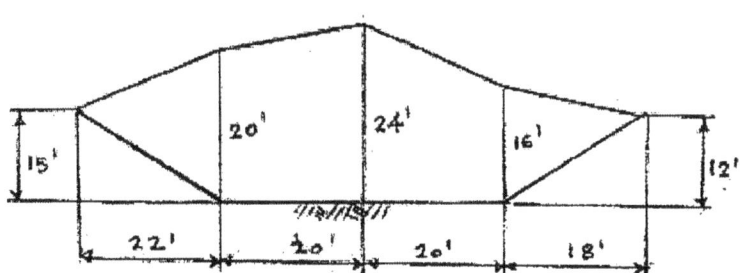

Shown above is the cut for a new highway at a given station. The area of the cut is _____ square feet.

A. 1204   B. 1224   C. 1244   D. 1264

16. The number of gallons of water in a cubic foot is

A. 7.33   B. 7.48   C. 8.00   D. 8.33

Questions 17-18.

DIRECTIONS: Questions 17 and 18 refer to a section across a city street.

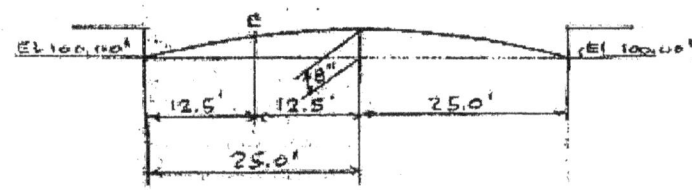

17. If the curve of the road is a parabola, the elevation of the road at point E is

A. 100.45   B. 100.50   C. 100.55   D. 100.60

18. The slope of "the road at E is _____ percent.

A. 2.00   B. 2.471   C. 2.667   D. 2.833

19. The universal lane width for a highway is _____ feet.

A. 10 to 11   B. 11 to 12   C. 12 to 13   D. 13 to 14

20. In unit price and lump sum contracts, contractors sometimes

A. reduce the unit price on items to be carried out early in the project and increase the unit price on items to be carried out later in the contract.
B. increase the unit price on items to be carried out early in the contract and reduce the unit price on items carried out later in the contract
C. reduce the unit price and increase the price on lump sum items
D. increase the price on unit items and decrease the price on lump sum items

Questions 21 to 23.

DIRECTIONS: Questions 21 to 23, inclusive, refer to the diagram below.

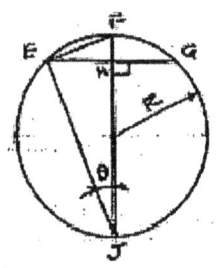

21. EF is equal to

    A. 2R sin θ   B. 2R cos θ   C. 2R tan θ   D. 2R cot θ

22. EH is equal to

    A. R sin 2θ   B. R cos 2θ   C. R tan 2θ   D. R cot 2θ

23. FH is equal to

    A. 2R sin θ cos θ/2
    C. 2R sin² θ
    B. 2R sin θ/2 cos θ
    D. 2R cos θ cos θ/2

24. The specifications state that the temperature shall be above 10° C. The temperature, in degrees Fahrenheit, is

    A. 40   B. 45   C. 50   D. 55

25. In a welding electrode designated by four numbers, the strength of the material in the electrode is shown in the _____ number(s).

    A. first
    C. first three
    B. first two
    D. four

KEY (CORRECT ANSWERS)

1. B
2. A
3. C
4. B
5. C

6. D
7. A
8. A
9. D
10. A

11. D
12. B
13. C
14. D
15. A

16. B
17. B
18. C
19. C
20. B

21. A
22. A
23. C
24. C
25. B

TEST 3

DIRECTIONS: Each question or incomplete statement is followed by several suggested answers or completions. Select the one that BEST answers the question or completes the statement. *PRINT THE LETTER OF THE CORRECT ANSWER IN THE SPACE AT THE RIGHT.*

1. Of the following elements, the one that is harmful in steel is 1.____

   A. molybdenum B. vandium
   C. silicon D. phosphorus

2. The size of a fillet weld shown at the right is designated by 2.____
   A. A
   B. B
   C. C
   D. D

3. The circle on the welding symbol means 3.____
   A. weld in shop
   B. weld in field
   C. plug weld
   D. weld all around

4. Stainless steel is designated as 18-8. The steel contains 4.____

   A. 18% vanadium, 8% chromium
   B. 18% chromium, 8% vanadium
   C. 18% nickel, 8% chromium
   D. 18% chromium, 8% nickel

5. Asphalt cements can be designated by one of two methods. One is viscosity, and the other is 5.____

   A. liquidity B. penetration
   C. elasticity D. ductility

6. Paving asphalts are measured by viscosity. A unit measure of absolute viscosity is 6.____

   A. poise   B. tesla   C. oersted   D. pascal

7. The one of the following solvents that is NOT used in cutback asphalt is 7.____

   A. naphtha   B. gasoline   C. toluene   D. kerosene

8. The advantage of using cutback asphalt over ordinary asphalt is that cutback asphalt _____ than ordinary asphalt. 8.____

   A. has a higher viscosity
   B. cures more slowly

C. can be applied at a temperature lower
D. produces a harder surfac

9. When excavating for a roadway, the volume of excavation removed becomes greater than the volume of the earth before removal. The percent of increase in volume is termed

   A. swell
   B. expansion
   C. blow-up
   D. displacement

10. The approximate increase in volume when dry sand is excavated is MOST NEARLY _____ percent.

    A. 2
    B. 20
    C. 28
    D. 36

11. The tolerance for the elevation of the base of a pavement is .02 feet. In the metric system, this would be

    A. ± 4
    B. ± 6
    C. ± 8
    D. ± 10

12. When the areas of a road surface to be patched are numerous, or they extend over a considerable area, it is often more efficient to recondition the entire surface. The usual procedure is to _____ the surface of the roadway to the full depth of the surface material.

    A. excavate
    B. eviscerate
    C. scarify
    D. plow

13. The ASTM defines a permeable textile material or any other geotechnical engineering-related material as a

    A. geomorphic material
    B. synthetic permeable textile
    C. geomorphic reinforcement
    D. geotextile

14. In wood terminology, a shake is a

    A. variation from a true or plane surface
    B. separation along the grain
    C. deviation edgewise from a straight line drawn from end to end of a piece
    D. lack of wood or bark from any cause

15. The primary difference between heartwood and sapwood is that

    A. heartwood is stronger than sapwood
    B. sapwood is stronger than heartwood
    C. sapwood is more susceptible to decay than heartwood
    D. sapwood is normally darker than heartwood

16. The specific gravity of southern yellow pine based on oven-dry weight and volume is

    A. .38
    B. .48
    C. G. .58
    D. .68

17. The length of a 10 penny nail is _____ inches.

    A. 3
    B. 3 1/4
    C. 3 1/2
    D. 4

18. The specifications state that in extreme situations face brick may be cleaned with a 5% solution of muriatic acid. Muriatic acid is another name for _____ acid.   18.____

    A. sulfuric
    B. hydrochloric
    C. acetic
    D. hydrofluoric

19. The main advantage of CPM over the traditional bar chart in scheduling a construction project is that CPM can more easily   19.____

    A. procure material
    B. eliminate potential bottlenecks during construction
    C. improve safety on the project
    D. eliminate unnecessary work to complete the project

20. In CPM, the float is   20.____

    A. positive in the critical path
    B. negative in the critical path
    C. 0 in the critical path
    D. positive or negative in the critical path, depending on whether the project is ahead of schedule or behind schedule

21. In CPM, the float in a given activity is the   21.____

    A. uncertainty when the activity can be finished without delaying the project
    B. uncertainty as to how much time is needed to complete the activity
    C. period during which the activity can be started without delaying the project
    D. flexibility needed to complete the activity without delaying the project

22. The GREATEST source of construction-related claims for additional payment for contractors and cost overruns result from   22.____

    A. labor strikes
    B. errors in design
    C. unanticipated soil conditions
    D. faulty material

23. High early strength cement is used in a concrete mix whenever the extra cost is offset by the value of the earlier use of the structure. The use of additional Portland cement in a mix gives high early strength, but has the disadvantage of   23.____

    A. causing segregation when placing the concrete
    B. having reduced strength over a longer period of time
    C. requires more fine aggregates
    D. causing greater shrinkage of the mass in curing

24. Special cements are designed specifically to resist chemical attack. The chemical group it is designed to resist are   24.____

    A. chlorates
    B. sulfates
    C. nitrates
    D. carbonates

25. Of the following, the synthetic fiber LEAST likely to raise loads in slings is 25._____

    A. nylon
    B. orlon
    C. polyester
    D. polypropylene

KEY (CORRECT ANSWERS)

1. D
2. C
3. D
4. D
5. B

6. A
7. C
8. C
9. A
10. A

11. B
12. C
13. D
14. B
15. C

16. C
17. A
18. B
19. B
20. C

21. C
22. C
23. D
24. B
25. B

TEST 4

DIRECTIONS: Each question or incomplete statement is followed by several suggested answers or completions. Select the one that BEST answers the question or completes the statement. *PRINT THE LETTER OF THE CORRECT ANSWER IN THE SPACE AT THE RIGHT.*

1. Of the following liquids, the one that has the LOWEST viscosity is

   A. alcohol
   B. water
   C. raw petroleum
   D. glycerin

   1.____

2. The inspector uses a sling psychrometer in check painting to check the

   A. density of the paint
   B. viscosity of the paint
   C. moisture in the air
   D. barometric pressure

   2.____

3. Of the following tests on structural steel, the one that is NOT non-destructive is

   A. radiographic
   B. ultrasonic
   C. magnetic particle
   D. tensile

   3.____

4. Which of the following is a high strength bolt?

   A. A7   B. A36   C. A325   D. A502

   4.____

5. The size of hole for a 3/4 inch bolt is

   A. 3/4"
   B. 13/32"
   C. 13/16"
   D. 27/32"

   5.____

6. Foam fire extinguishers are unsuitable to fight _____ fires.

   A. wood
   B. paper
   C. flammable liquid
   D. electric equipment

   6.____

7. Of the following types of fire extinguishers, the one MOST suitable to fight wood and paper fires is

   A. water type-soda acid
   B. carbon dioxide
   C. sodium bicarbonate-dry chemical
   D. potassium bicarbonate-dry chemical

   7.____

8. A multi-purpose fire extinguisher is

   A. foam
   B. carbon dioxide
   C. ABC
   D. soda acid

   8.____

9. The fire extinguisher with the SHORTEST range is

   9.____

A. cartridge operated B. soda acid
C. carbon dioxide D. stored pressure

10. The Occupational Safety and Health Act Part 1926 states that all trenches and earth embankments over _____ feet deep beoadequately protected against caving in.

    A. 4 B. 5 C. 6 D. 7

11. During excavation, most cave-ins occur

    A. when excavating for retaining walls
    B. during cold weather
    C. in shallow excavations
    D. in the western part of the United States

12. _____ soils are MOST susceptible to cave-ins.

    A. All B. Clayey C. Silty D. Sandy

13. In highway construction work, material required for earthwork construction in excess of the quantity of suitable material available from the required grading, cuts and elevations is known as

    A. overhaul B. deficit
    C. borrow D. shrinkage

14. The number of strands in manila rope is USUALLY

    A. 2 B. 3 C. 4 D. 5

15. The factor of safety for manila rope is

    A. 3 B. 5 C. 7 D. 9

Questions 16-20.

DIRECTIONS: Questions 16 through 20, inclusive, refer to a section through a 20'-0" long reinforced concrete retaining wall.

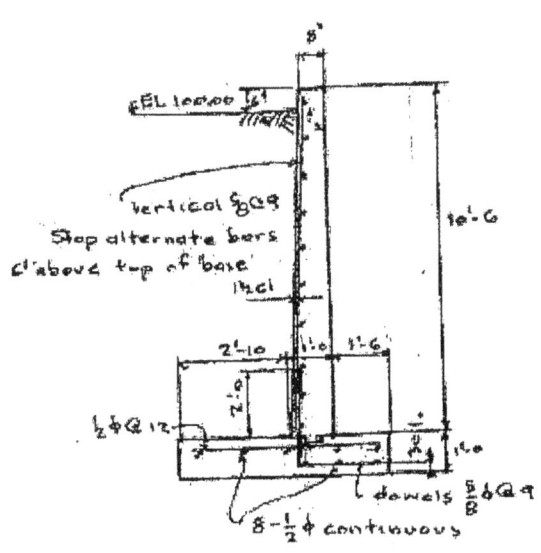

16. The slope of the inclined wall is MOST NEARLY

    A. 1/8 inch on 12"
    B. 1/4 inch on 12"
    C. 3/8 inch on 12"
    D. 1/2 inch on 12"

17. The volume of concrete in the vertical wall is _____ _____ cubic yards.

    A. 5.9   B. 6.1   C. 6.3   D. 6.5

18. The elevation of the bottom of the footing is

    A. 89.00'   B. 89.500'   C. 90.00'   D. 90.5'

19. The number of dowels ' a is

    A. 23   B. 25   C. 27   D. 29

20. The number of vertical '-a that are the full height of the wall is

    A. 12   B. 14   C. 16   D. 27

21. A state highway contract contains a Buy America clause. The material referred to in the clause is MOST NEARLY

    A. cement
    B. lumber
    C. aluminum
    D. steel

22. In a unit price contract where additional work does not fall under any item, the extra work is to be paid on a cost-plus basis. If the contractor uses his own crane, he is entitled to the

    A. cost of operating the crane only
    B. cost of operating the crane and servicing the crane only
    C. rental cost of the crane, the cost of operating the crane, and the cost of servicing the crane only
    D. cost of repairing the crane if the crane is damaged and the cost of operating and servicing the crane only

23. The delivery ticket for a truck delivering bituminous pavement mixture contains an entry "Tare Weight." Tare weight on the ticket refers to the

    A. correction for the scales weighing the bituminous mixture
    B. truck weight without load
    C. weight of fuel on the truck
    D. truck weight with load

24. The PRIMARY difference between silt and loam is that

    A. silt contains some organic material
    B. loam contains some organic material
    C. silt consists primarily of clay
    D. loam consists primarily of clay

25. A recent development in high strength concrete is _____ concrete. 25.____
   A. silica fume
   B. low slump
   C. fly ash
   D. finely ground cement

KEY (CORRECT ANSWERS)

1.	A	11.	C
2.	C	12.	A
3.	D	13.	C
4.	C	14.	B
5.	B	15.	B
6.	D	16.	C
7.	A	17.	D
8.	C	18.	A
9.	C	19.	C
10.	B	20.	B

21. D
22. C
23. B
24. B
25. A

EXAMINATION SECTION
TEST 1

DIRECTIONS: Each question or incomplete statement is followed by several suggested answers or completions. Select the one that BEST answers the question or completes the statement. *PRINT THE LETTER OF THE CORRECT ANSWER IN THE SPACE AT THE RIGHT.*

1. A *basic* method of operation that a *good* supervisor should follow is to

    A. check the work of subordinates constantly to make sure they are not making exceptions to the rules
    B. train subordinates so they can handle problems that come up regularly themselves and come to him only with special cases
    C. delegate to subordinates only those duties which he cannot do himself
    D. issue directions to subordinates only on special matters

2. To do a *good* job of performance evaluation, it is BEST for a supervisor to

    A. compare the employee's performance to that of another employee doing similar work
    B. give greatest weight to instances of unusually good or unusually poor performance
    C. leave out any consideration of the employee's personal traits
    D. measure the employee's performance against standard performance requirements

3. Of the following, the MOST important reason for a supervisor to have private face to face discussions with subordinates about their performance is to

    A. help employees improve their work
    B. give special praise to employees who perform well
    C. encourage the employees to compete for higher performance ratings
    D. discipline employees who perform poorly

4. Of the following, the CHIEF purpose of a probationary period for a new employee is to allow time for

    A. finding out whether the selection processes are satisfactory
    B. the employee to make adjustments in his home circumstances made necessary by the job
    C. the employee to decide whether he wants a permanent appointment
    D. determining the fitness of the employee to continue in the job

5. When a subordinate resigns his job, it is MOST important to conduct an exit interview in order to

    A. try to get the employee to remain on the job
    B. learn the true reasons for the employee's resignation
    C. see that the employee leaves with a good opinion of the agency
    D. ask the employee if he would consider a transfer

6. Chronic lateness of employees is generally LEAST likely to be due to

    A. distance of job location from home   B. poor personnel administration
    C. unexpressed employee grievances   D. low morale

7. Of the following, the LEAST effective stimulus for motivating employees toward inproved performance over a long-range period is

   A. their sense of achievement
   B. their feeling of recognition
   C. opportunity for their self-development
   D. an increase in salary

8. Suppose that NOT ONE of a group of employees has turned in an idea to the employees suggestion system during the past year.
   The *most probable* reason for this situation is that the

   A. money awards given for suggestions used are not high enough to make employees interested
   B. employees in this group are not able to develop any good ideas
   C. supervisor of these employees is not doing enough to encourage them to take part in the program
   D. methods and procedures of operation do not need improvement

9. A subordinate tells you that he is having trouble concentrating on his work due to a personal problem at home.
   Of the following, it would be BEST for you to

   A. refer him to a community service agency
   B. listen quietly to the story because he may just need a sympathetic ear
   C. tell him that you cannot help him because the problem is not job related
   D. ask him questions about the nature of the problem and tell him how you would handle it

10. For you as a supervisor to give each of your subordinates *exactly* the same type of supervision is

    A. *advisable*, because doing this insures fair and impartial treatment of each individual
    B. *not advisable*, because individuals like to think that they are receiving better treatment than others
    C. *advisable*, because once a supervisor learns how to deal with a subordinate who brings a problem to him, he can handle another subordinate with this problem in the same way
    D. *not advisable*, because each person is different and there is no one supervisory procedure for dealing with individuals that applies in every case

11. A senior employee under your supervision tells you that he is reluctant to speak to one of his subordinates about his poor work habits, because this worker is "strong-willed" and he does not want to antagonize him.
    For you to offer to speak to the subordinate about this matter yourself would be

    A. *advisable*, since you are in a position of greater authority
    B. *inadvisable*, since handling this problem is a basic supervisory responsibility of the senior employee
    C. *advisable*, since the senior employee must work more closely with the worker than you do
    D. *inadvisable*, since you should not risk antagonizing the employee yourself

12. Some of your subordinates have been coming to you with complaints you feel are unimportant. For you to hear their stories out is

    A. *poor practice,* you should spend your time on more important matters
    B. *good practice,* this will increase your popularity with your subordinates
    C. *poor practice,* subordinates should learn to come to you only with major grievances
    D. *good practice,* it may prevent minor complaints from developing into major grievances

13. Assume that an agency has an established procedure for handling employee grievances. An employee in this agency, comes to his immediate supervisor with a grievance. The supervisor investigates the matter and makes a decision.
    However, the employee is not satisfied with the decision made by the supervisor. The BEST action for the supervisor to take is to

    A. tell the employee he will review the matter further
    B. remind the employee that he is the supervisor and the employee must act in accordance with his decision
    C. explain to the employee how he can carry his complaint forward to the next step in the grievance procedure
    D. tell the employee he will consult with his own superiors on the matter

14. Subordinate employees and senior employees often must make quick decisions while in the field. The supervisor can BEST help subordinates meet such situations by

    A. training them in the appropriate action to take for every problem that may come up
    B. limiting the areas in which they are permitted to make decisions
    C. making certain they understand clearly the basic policies of the bureau and the department
    D. delegating authority to make such decisions to only a few subordinates on each level

15. Studies have shown that the CHIEF cause of failure to achieve success as a supervisor is

    A. an unwillingness to delegate authority to subordinates
    B. the establishment of high performance standards for subordinates
    C. the use of discipline that is too strict
    D. showing too much leniency to poor workers

16. When a supervisor delegates to a subordinate certain work that he normally does himself, it is MOST important that he give the subordinate

    A. responsibility for also setting the standards for the work to be done
    B. sufficient authority to be able to carry out the assignment
    C. written, step-by-step instructions for doing the work
    D. an explanation of one part of the task at a time

17. It is particularly important that disciplinary actions be equitable as between individuals. This statement *implies* that

    A. punishment applied in disciplinary actions should be lenient
    B. proposed disciplinary actions should be reviewed by higher authority
    C. subordinates should have an opportunity to present their stories before penalties are applied
    D. penalties for violations of the rules should be standardized and consistently applied

18. You discover that from time to time a number of false rumors circulate among your subordinates.
    Of the following, the BEST way for you to handle this situation is to

    A. ignore the rumors since rumors circulate in every office and can never be eliminated
    B. attempt to find those responsible for the rumors and reprimand them
    C. make sure that your employees are informed as soon as possible about all matters that affect them
    D. inform your superior about the rumors and let him deal with the matter

19. Supervisors who allow the "halo effect" to influence their evaluations of subordinates are *most likely* to

    A. give more lenient ratings to older employees who have longer service
    B. let one highly favorable or unfavorable trait unduly affect their judgment of an employee
    C. evaluate all employees on one trait before considering a second
    D. give high evaluations in order to avoid antagonizing their subordinates

20. For a supervisor to keep records of reprimands to subordinates about infractions of the rules is

    A. *good practice,* because these records are valuable to support disciplinary actions recommended or taken
    B. *poor practice,* because such records are evidence of the supervisor's inability to maintain discipline
    C. *good practice,* because such records indicate that the supervisor is doing a good job
    D. *poor practice,* because the best way to correct subordinates is to give them more training

21. When a new departmental policy has been established, it would be MOST advisable for you, as a supervisor, to

    A. distribute a memo which states the new policy and instruct your subordinates to read it
    B. explain specifically to your subordinates how the policy is going to affect them
    C. make sure your subordinates understand that you are not responsible for setting the policy
    D. tell your subordinates whether you agree or disagree with the policy

22. As a supervisor, you receive several complaints about the rude conduct of a subordinate. 22.____
    The FIRST action you should take is to
    A. request his transfer to another office
    B. prepare a charge sheet for disciplinary action
    C. assign a senior employee to work with him for a week
    D. interview the employee to determine possible reason, and warn that correction is necessary

23. A supervisor is *most likely* to get subordinates to work cooperatively toward accomplishing bureau goals if he 23.____
    A. creates an atmosphere that contributes to their feeling of security
    B. backs up subordinates even when they occasionally disobey regulations
    C. shows interest in subordinates by helping them solve their personal problems
    D. uses an authoritarian or "bossy" approach to supervision

24. A supervisor is holding a staff meeting with his senior employees to try to find an acceptable solution to a problem that has come up. 24.____
    Of the following, the CHIEF role of the supervisor at this meeting should be to
    A. see that every member of the group contributes at least one suggestions
    B. act as chairman of the meeting, but take no other active part to avoid influencing the senior employees
    C. keep the participants from wandering off into discussions of irrelevant matters
    D. make certain the participants hear his views on the matter at the beginning of the meeting

25. An employee shows you a certificate that he has just received for completing two years of study in conversational Spanish. As his supervisor, it would be BEST for you to 25.____
    A. put a note about this accomplishment in his personnel folder
    B. assign him to areas in which people of Spanish origin live
    C. congratulate him on this accomplishment, but tell him frankly that you doubt this is likely to have any direct bearing on his work
    D. encourage him to continue his studies and become thoroughly fluent in speaking the language

KEY (CORRECT ANSWERS)

1.	B	11.	B
2.	D	12.	D
3.	A	13.	C
4.	D	14.	C
5.	B	15.	A
6.	A	16.	B
7.	D	17.	D
8.	C	18.	C
9.	B	19.	B
10.	D	20.	A

21. B
22. D
23. A
24. C
25. A

TEST 2

DIRECTIONS: Each question or incomplete statement is followed by several suggested answers or completions. Select the one that BEST answers the question or completes the statement. *PRINT THE LETTER OF THE CORRECT ANSWER IN THE SPACE AT THE RIGHT.*

1. Of the following, the factor affecting employee morale which the immediate supervisor is LEAST able to control is

    A. handling of grievances
    B. fair and impartial treatment of subordinates
    C. general presonnel rules and regulations
    D. accident prevention

    1.____

2. When one of your workers does outstanding work, you should

    A. explain to your other employees that you expect the same kind of work of them
    B. praise him for his work so that he will know it is appreciated
    C. say nothing, because other employees may think you are showing favoritism
    D. show him how his work can be improved still more so that he will not sit back

    2.____

3. For you as a supervisor to consider a suggestion from a probationary worker for improving a procedure would be

    A. *poor practice,* because this employee is too new on the job to know much about it
    B. *good practice,* because you may be able to share credit for the suggestion
    C. *poor practice,* because it may hurt the morale of the older employees
    D. *good practice,* because the suggestion may be worthwhile

    3.____

4. If you find you must criticize the work of one of your workers, it would be BEST for you to

    A. mention the good points in his work as well as the faults
    B. caution him that he will receive an unsatisfactory performance report unless his work improves
    C. compare his work to that of the other agents you supervise
    D. apologize for making the criticism

    4.____

5. As a senior employee which one of the following matters would it be BEST for you to talk over with your supervisor before you take final action?

    A. One of the workers you supervise continues to disregard your instructions repeatedly in spite of repeated warnings
    B. One of your workers tells you he wants to discuss a personal problem
    C. A probationary employee tells you he does not understand a procedure
    D. One of your workers tells you he disagrees with the way you rate his work

    5.____

6. If one of your subordinates asks you a question about a department rule and you do not know the answer, you should tell him that

    A. he should try to get the information himself
    B. you do not have the answer, but you will get it for him as soon as you can
    C. he should ask you the question again a week from now
    D. he should put the question in writing

    6.____

7. If, as a supervisor, you realize that you have been unfair in criticizing one of your subordinates, the BEST action for you to take is to

   A. say nothing, but overlook some error made by this employee in the future
   B. be frank and tell the employee that you are sorry for the mistake you made
   C. let the employee know in some indirect way without admitting your mistake, that you realize he was not at fault
   D. say nothing, but be more careful about criticizing subordinates in the future

8. Of the following, the MOST important reason for a supervisor to write an accident report as soon as possible after an accident has happened is to

   A. make sure that important facts about the accident are not forgotten
   B. avoid delay in getting compensation for the injured person
   C. get adequate medical treatment for the injured person
   D. keep department accident statistics up to date

9. In any matter which may require disciplinary action, the FIRST responsibility of the supervisor is to

   A. decide what penalty should be applied for the offense
   B. refer the matter to a higher authority for complete investigation
   C. place the interests of the department above those of the employee
   D. investigate the matter fully to get all the facts

10. Suppose you find it necessary to criticize one of the subordinates you supervise. You should

    A. send an official letter to his home
    B. speak to him about the matter privately
    C. speak to him at a staff meeting
    D. ask another worker who is friendly with him to talk to him about the matter

11. Some of your subordinates have been coming to you with complaints you feel are unimportant. For you to hear their stories out is

    A. *poor practice,* you should spend your time on more important matters
    B. *good practice,* this will increase your popularity with your subordinates
    C. *poor practice,* subordinates should learn to come to you only with major grievances
    D. *good practice,* it may prevent minor complaints from developing into major grievances

12. Suppose that NOT ONE of a group of employees has turned in an idea to the employees' suggestion system during the past year. The *most probable* reason for this situation is that the

    A. supervisor of these employees is not doing enough to encourage them to take part in this program
    B. employees in this group are not able to develop any good ideas
    C. money awards given for suggestions used are not high enough to make employees interested
    D. methods and procedures of operation do not need improvement

13. For you as a supervisor to give each of your subordinates *exactly* the same type of supervision is

    A. *advisable,* because doing this insures fair and impartial treatment of each individual
    B. *not advisable,* because each person is different and there is no one supervisory procedure for dealing with individuals that applies in every case
    C. *advisable,* because once a supervisor learns how to deal with a subordinate who brings a problem to him, he can handle another subordinate with this problem in the same way
    D. *not advisable,* because individuals like to think that they are receiving better treatment than others

14. In evaluating personnel, a supervisor should keep in mind that the MOST important objective of performance evaluations is to

    A. encourage employees to compete for higher performance ratings
    B. give recognition to employees who perform well
    C. help employees improve their work
    D. discipline employees who perform poorly

15. A subordinate tells you that he is having trouble concentrating on his work due to a personal problem at home. Of the following, it would be BEST for you to

    A. refer him to a community service agency
    B. listen quietly to the story because he may just need a sympathetic ear
    C. tell him that you cannot help him because the problem is not job-related
    D. ask him some questions about the nature of the problem and tell him how you would handle it

16. To do a good job of performance evaluation, it is BEST for a supervisor to

    A. measure the employee's performance against standard performance requirements
    B. compare the employee's performance to that of another employee doing similar work
    C. leave out any consideration of the employee's personal traits
    D. give greatest weight to instances of unusually good or unusually poor performance

17. It is particularly important that disciplinary actions be equitable as between individuals. This statement *implies* that

    A. punishment applied in disciplinary actions should be lenient
    B. proposed disciplinary actions should be reviewed by higher authority
    C. subordinates should have an opportunity to present their stories before penalties are applied
    D. penalties for violations of the rules should be standardized and consistently applied

18. Assume that an agency has an established procedure for handling employee grievances. An employee in this agency comes to his immediate supervisor with a grievance. The supervisor investigates the matter and makes a decision. However, the employee is not satisfied with the decision made by the supervisor.
    The BEST action for the supervisor to take is to

A. tell the employee he will review the matter further
B. remind the employee that he is the supervisor and the employee must act in accordance with his decision
C. explain to the employee how he can carry his complaint forward to the next step in the grievance procedure
D. tell the employee he will consult with his own superiors on the matter

19. Of the following, the CHIEF purpose of a probationary period for a new employee is to allow time for

    A. finding out whether the selection processes are satisfactory
    B. determining the fitness of the employee to continue in the job
    C. the employee to decide whether he wants a permanent appointment
    D. the employee to make adjustments in his home circumstances made necessary by the job

20. Of the following, the subject that would be MOST important to include in a "break-in" program for new employees is

    A. explanation of rules, regulations and policies of the agency
    B. Instruction in the agency's history and programs
    C. explanation of the importance of the new employees' own particular job
    D. explanation of the duties and responsibilities of the employee

21. Suppose a new employee under your supervision seems slow to learn and is making mistakes in performing his duties. Your FIRST action should be to

    A. pass this information on to the bureau director
    B. reprimand the worker so he will not repeat these mistakes
    C. find out whether this worker understands your instructions
    D. note these facts for future reference when writing up the monthly performance evaluation

22. In training new employees to do a certain job it would be LEAST desirable for you to

    A. demonstrate how the job is done, step by step
    B. encourage the workers to ask questions if they aren't clear about any point
    C. tell them about the various mistakes other agents have made in doing this job
    D. have the workers do the job, explaining to you what they are doing and why

23. One of the workers under your supervision is resentful when you ask her to remove her jangling bracelets before she starts her tour of duty.
    Of the following, the BEST explanation you can give her for the rule against wearing such jewelry while on duty is that

    A. the jewelry may create a safety hazard
    B. employees must give up certain personal liberties if they want to keep their jobs
    C. workers cannot perform their duties as efficiently if they wear distracting jewelry
    D. citizens may receive an unfavorable impression of the department

24. Of the following, the LEAST important reason for having a department handbook and a bureau standard operating procedure is to

    A. help in training new employees
    B. provide a source of reference for department and bureau rules and procedures
    C. prevent errors in work by providing clear guidelines
    D. make the supervisor's job easy

25. On inspecting your squad prior to their tour of duty, you note an employee improperly and unacceptably dressed.
    The FIRST action you should take is to

    A. call the employee aside and insist on immediate correction if possible
    B. notify the district commander right away
    C. have the employee submit a memorandum explaining the reason for the improper uniform
    D. permit the employee to proceed on duty but warn him not to let this happen again

KEY (CORRECT ANSWERS)

1.	C	11.	D
2.	B	12.	A
3.	D	13.	B
4.	A	14.	C
5.	A	15.	B
6.	B	16.	A
7.	B	17.	D
8.	A	18.	C
9.	D	19.	B
10.	B	20.	D

21.	C
22.	C
23.	D
24.	D
25.	A

SUPERVISION STUDY GUIDE

Social science has developed information about groups and leadership in general and supervisor-employee relationships in particular. Since organizational effectiveness is closely linked to the ability of supervisors to direct the activities of employees, these findings are important to executives everywhere.

IS A SUPERVISOR A LEADER?

First-line supervisors are found in all large business and government organizations. They are the men at the base of an organizational hierarchy. Decisions made by the head of the organization reach them through a network of intermediate positions. They are frequently referred to as part of the management team, but their duties seldom seem to support this description.

A supervisor of clerks, tax collectors, meat inspectors, or securities analysts is not charged with budget preparation. He cannot hire or fire the employees in his own unit on his say-so. He does not administer programs which require great planning, coordinating, or decision making.

Then what is he? He is the man who is directly in charge of a group of employees doing productive work for a business or government agency. If the work requires the use of machines, the men he supervises operate them. If the work requires the writing of reports, the men he supervises write them. He is expected to maintain a productive flow of work without creating problems which higher levels of management must solve. But is he a leader?

To carry out a specific part of an agency's mission, management creates a unit, staffs it with a group of employees and designates a supervisor to take charge of them. Management directs what this unit shall do, from time to time changes directions, and often indicates what the group should not do. Management presumably creates status for the supervisor by giving him more pay, a title, and special privileges.

Management asks a supervisor to get his workers to attain organizational goals, including the desired quantity and quality of production. Supposedly, he has authority to enable him to achieve this objective. Management at least assumes that by establishing the status of the supervisor's position, it has created sufficient authority to enable him to achieve these goals—not his goals, nor necessarily the group's, but management's goals.

In addition, supervision includes writing reports, keeping records of membership in a higher-level administrative group, industrial engineering, safety engineering, editorial duties, housekeeping duties, etc. The supervisor as a member of an organizational network, must be responsible to the changing demands of the management above him. At the same time, he must be responsive to the demands of the work group of which he is a member. He is placed in the difficult position of communicating and implementing new decisions, changed programs and revised production quotas for his work group, although he may have had little part in developing them.

It follows, then, that supervision has a special characteristic: achievement of goals, previously set by management, through the efforts of others. It is in this feature of the supervisor's job that we find the role of a leader in the sense of the following definition: *A leader is that person who most effectively influences group activities toward goal setting and goal achievements.*

This definition is broad. It covers both leaders in groups that come together voluntarily and in those brought together through a work assignment in a factory, store, or government agency. In the natural group, the authority necessary to attain goals is determined by the group membership and is granted by them. In the working group, it is apparent that the establishment of a supervisory position creates a predisposition on the part of employees to accept the authority of the occupant of that position. We cannot, however, assume that mere occupation confers authority sufficient to assure the accomplishment of an organization's goals.

Supervision is different, then, from leadership. The supervisor is expected to fulfill the role of leader but without obtaining a grant of authority from the group he supervises. The supervisor is expected to influence the group in the achieving of goals but is often handicapped by having little influence on the organizational process by which goals are set. The supervisor, because he works in an organizational setting, has the burdens of additional organizational duties and restrictions and requirements arising out of the fact that his position is subordinate to a hierarchy of higher-level supervisors. These differences between leadership and supervision are reflected in our definition: *Supervision is basically a leadership role, in a formal organization, which has as its objective the effective influencing of other employees.*

Even though these differences between supervision and leadership exist, a significant finding of experimenters in this field is that supervisors must be leaders to be successful.

The problem is: How can a supervisor exercise leadership in an organizational setting? We might say that the supervisor is expected to be a natural leader in a situation which does not come about naturally. His situation becomes really difficult in an organization which is more eager to make its supervisors into followers rather than leaders.

LEADERSHIP: NATURAL AND ORGANIZATIONAL

Leadership, in its usual sense of *natural* leadership, and supervision are not the same. In some cases, leadership embraces broader powers and functions than supervision; in other cases, supervision embraces more than leadership. This is true both because of the organization and technical aspects of the supervisor's job and because of the relatively freer setting and inherent authority of the natural leader.

The natural leader usually has much more authority and influence than the supervisor. Group members not only follow his command but prefer it that way. The employee, however, can appeal the supervisor's commands to his union or to the supervisor's superior or to the personnel office. These intercessors represent restrictions on the supervisor's power to lead.

The natural leader can gain greater membership involvement in the group's objectives, and he can change the objectives of the group. The supervisor can attempt to gain employee support only for management's objectives; he cannot set other objectives. In these instances leadership is broader than supervision.

The natural leader must depend upon whatever skills are available when seeking to attain objectives. The supervisor is trained in the administrative skills necessary to achieve management's goals. If he does not possess the requisite skills, however, he can call upon management's technicians.

A natural leader can maintain his leadership, in certain groups, merely by satisfying members' need for group affiliation. The supervisor must maintain his leadership by directing and organizing his group to achieve specific organizational goals set for him and his group by management. He must have a technical competence and a kind of coordinating ability which is not needed by many natural leaders.

A natural leader is responsible only to his group which grants him authority. The supervisor is responsible to management, which employs him, and also to the work group of which he is a member. The supervisor has the exceedingly difficult job of reconciling the demands of two groups frequently in conflict. He is often placed in the untenable position of trying to play two antagonistic roles. In the above instance, supervision is broader than leadership.

ORGANIZATIONAL INFLUENCES ON LEADERSHIP

The supervisor is both a product and a prisoner of the organization wherein we find him. The organization which creates the supervisor's position also obstructs, restricts, and channelizes the exercise of his duties. These influences extend beyond prescribed functional relationships to specific supervisory behavior. For example, even in a face-to-face situation involving one of his subordinates, the supervisor's actions are controlled to a great extent by his organization. His behavior must conform to the organization policy on human relations, rules which dictate personnel procedures, specific prohibitions governing conduct, the attitudes of his own superior, etc. He is not a free agent operating within the limits of his work group. His freedom of action is much more circumscribed than is generally admitted. The organizational influences which limit his leadership actions can be classified as structure, prescriptions, and proscriptions.

The organizational structure places each supervisor's position in context with other designated positions. It determines the relationships between his position and specific positions which impinge on his. The structure of the organization designates a certain position to which he looks for orders and information about his work. It gives a particular status to his position within a pattern of statuses from which he perceives that (1) certain positions are on a par, organizationally, with his, (2) other positions are subordinate, and (3) still others are superior.

The organizational structure determines those positions to which he should look for advice and assistance, and those positions to which he should give advice and assistance.

For instance, the organizational structure has predetermined that the supervisor of a clerical processing unit shall report to a supervisory position in a higher echelon. He shall have certain relationships with the supervisors of the work units which transmit work to and receive work from his unit. He shall discuss changes and clarification of procedures with certain staff units, such as organization and methods, cost accounting, and personnel. He shall consult supervisors of units which provide or receive special work assignments.

The organizational structure, however, establishes patterns other than those of the relationships of positions. These are the patterns of responsibility, authority, and expectations.

The supervisor is responsible for certain activities or results; he is presumably invested with the authority to achieve these. His set of authority and responsibility is interwoven with other sets to the end that all goals and functions of the organization are parceled out in small, manageable lots. This, of course, establishes a series of expectations: a single supervisor can perform his particular set of duties only upon the assumption that preceding or contiguous sets of duties have been, or are being carried out. At the same time, he is aware of the expectations of others that he will fulfill his functional role.

The structure of an organization establishes relationships between specified positions and specific expectations for these positions. The fact that these relationships and expectations are established is one thing; whether or not they are met is another.

PRESCRIPTIONS AND PROSCRIPTIONS

But let us return to the organizational influences which act to restrict the supervisor's exercise of leadership. These are the prescriptions and proscriptions generally in effect in all organizations, and those peculiar to a single organization. In brief these are the *thou shalt's* and the *thou shalt not's*.

Organizations not only prescribe certain duties for individual supervisory positions, they also prescribe specific methods and means of carrying out these duties and maintaining management-employee relations. These include rules, regulations, policy, and tradition. It does no good for the supervisor to say, *This seems to be the best way to handle such-and-such,* if the organization has established a routine for dealing with problems. For good or bad, there are rules that state that firings shall be executed in such a manner, accompanied by a certain notification; that training shall be conducted, and in this manner. Proscriptions are merely negative prescriptions; you may not discriminate against any employee because of politics or race; you shall not suspend any employee without following certain procedures and obtaining certain approvals.

Most of these prohibitions and rules apply to the area of interpersonal relations, precisely the area which is now arousing most interest on the part of administrators and managers. We have become concerned about the contrast between formally prescribed relationships and interpersonal relationships, and this brings us to the often discussed informal organization.

FORMAL AND INFORMAL ORGANIZATIONS

As we well know, the functions and activities of any organization are broken down into individual units of work called positions. Administrators must establish a pattern which will link these positions to each other and relate them to a system of authority and responsibility. Man-to-man are spelled out as plainly as possible for all to understand. Managers, then, build an official structure which we call the formal organization.

In these same organizations, employees react individually and in groups to institutionally determined roles. John, a worker, rides in the same carpool as Joe, a foreman. An unplanned communication develops. Harry, a machinist knows more about high-speed machining than his foreman or anyone else in his shop. An unofficial tool boss comes into being. Mary, who fought with Jane, is promoted over her. Jane now gives Mary's directions. A planned relationship fails to develop. The employees have built a structure which we call the informal organization.

Formal organization is a system of management-prescribed relations between positions in an organization.

Informal organization is a network of unofficial relations between people in an organization.

These definitions might lead us to the absurd conclusion that positions carry out formal activities and that employe4es spend their time in unofficial activities. We must recognize that organizational activities are in all cases carried out by people. The formal structure provides a needed framework within which interpersonal relations occur. What we call informal organization is the complex of normal, natural relations among employees. These personal relationships may be negative or positive. That is, they may impede or aid the achievement of organizational goals. For example, friendship between two supervisors greatly increases the probability of good cooperation and coordination between their sections. On the other hand, *buck passing* nullifies the formal structure by failure to meet a prescribed and expected responsibility.

It is improbable that an ideal organization exists where all activities are carried out in strict conformity to a formally prescribed pattern of functional roles. Informal organization arises because of the incompleteness and ambiguities in the network of formally prescribed relationships, or in response to the needs or inadequacies of supervisors or managers who hold prescribed functional roles in an organization. Many of these relationships are not prescribed by the organizational pattern; many cannot be prescribed; many should not be prescribed.

Management faces the problem of keeping the informal organization in harmony with the mission of the agency. One way to do this is to make sure that all employees have a clear understanding of and are sympathetic with that mission. The issuance of organizational charts, procedural manuals, and functional descriptions of the work to be done by divisions and sections helps communicate management's plans and goals. Issuances alone, of course, cannot do the whole job. They should be accompanied by oral discussion and explanation. Management must ensure that there is mutual understanding and acceptance of charts and procedures. More important is that management acquaint itself with the attitudes, activities, and peculiar brands of logic which govern the informal organization. Only through this type of knowledge can they and supervisors keep informal goals consistent with the agency mission.

SUPERVISION STATUS AND FUNCTIONAL ROLE

A well-established supervisor is respected by the employees who work with him. They defer to his wishes. It is clear that a superior-subordinate relationship has been established. That is, status of the supervisor has been established in relation to other employees of the same work group. This same supervisor gains the respect of employees when he behaves in as certain manner. He will be expected, generally, to follow the customs of the group in such matters as dress, recreation, and manner of speaking. The group has a set of expectations as to his behavior. His position is a functional role which carries with it a collection of rights and obligations.

The position of supervisor usually has a status distinct from the individual who occupies it: it is much like a position description which exists whether or not there is an incumbent. The status of a supervisory position is valued higher than that of an employee position both because of the functional role of leadership which is assigned to it and because of the status symbols of titles, rights, and privileges which go with it.

Social ranking, or status, is not simple because it involves both the position and the man. An individual may be ranked higher than others because of his education, social background, perceived leadership ability, or conformity to group customs and ideals. If such a man is ranked higher by the members of a work group than their supervisor, the supervisor's effectiveness may be seriously undermined.

If the organization does not build and reinforce a supervisor's status, his position can be undermined in a different way. This will happen when managers go around rather than through the supervisor or designate him as a straw boss, acting boss, or otherwise not a real boss.

Let us clarify this last point. A role, and corresponding status, establishes a set of expectations. Employees expect their supervisor to do certain things and to act in certain ways. They are prepared to respond to that expected behavior. When the supervisor's behavior does not conform to their expectations, they are surprised, confused, and ill-at-ease. It becomes necessary for them to resolve their confusion, if they can. They might do this by turning to one of their own members for leadership. If the confusion continues, or their attempted solutions are not satisfactory, they will probably become a poorly motivated, non-cohesive group which cannot function very well.

COMMUNICATION AND THE SUPERVISOR

In a recent survey, railroad workers reported that they rarely look to their supervisor for information about the company. This is startling, at least to us, because we ordinarily think of the supervisor as the link between management and worker. We expect the supervisor to be the prime source of information about the company. Actually, the railroad workers listed the supervisor next to last in the o5rder of their sources of information. Most surprising of all, the supervisors, themselves, stated that rumor and unofficial contacts were their principal sources of information. Here we see one of the reasons why supervisors may not be as effective as management desires.

The supervisor is not only being bypassed by his work group, he is being ignored, and his position weakened, by the very organization which is holding him responsible for the activities of his workers. If he is management's representative to the employee, then management has an obligation to keep him informed of its activities. This is necessary if he is to carry out his functions efficiently and maintain his leadership in the work group. The supervisor is expected to be a source of information; when he is not, his status is not clear, and employees are dissatisfied because he has not lived up to expectations.

By providing information to the supervisor to pass along to employees, we can strengthen his position as leader of the group, and increase satisfaction and cohesion within the group. Because he has more information than the other members, receives information sooner, and passes it along at the proper times, members turn to him as a source and also provide him with information in the hope of receiving some in return. From this, we can see an increase in group cohesiveness because:

- Employees are bound closer to their supervisor because he is *in the know*.
- There is less need to go outside the group for answers
- Employees will more quickly turn to the supervisor for enlightenment

The fact that he has the answers will also enhance the supervisor's standing in the eyes of his men. This increased status will serve to bolster his authority and control of the group and will probably result in improved morale and productivity.

The foregoing, of course, does not mean that all management information should be given out. There are obviously certain policy determinations and discussions which need not or cannot be transmitted to all supervisors. However, the supervisor must be kept as fully informed as possible so that he can answer questions when asked and can allay needless fears and anxieties. Further, the supervisor has the responsibility of encouraging employee questions and submissions of information. He must be able to present information to employees so that it is clearly understood and accepted. His attitude and manner should make it clear that he believes in what he is saying, that the information is necessary or desirable to the group, and that he is prepared to act on the basis of the information.

SUPERVISION AND JOB PERFORMANCE

The productivity of work groups is a product; employees' efforts are multiplied by the supervision they receive. Many investigators have analyzed this relationship and have discovered elements of supervision which differentiate high and low production groups. These researchers have identified certain types of supervisory practices which they classify as *employee-centered* and other types which they classify as *production centered*.

The difference between these two kinds of supervision lies not in specific practices but in the approach or orientation to supervision. The employee-centered supervisor directs most of his efforts toward increasing employee motivation. He is concerned more with realizing the potential energy of persons than with administrative and technological methods of increasing efficiency and productivity. He is the man who finds ways of causing employees to want to work harder with the same tools. These supervisors emphasize the personal relations between their employees and themselves.

Now, obviously, these pictures are overdrawn. No one supervisor has all the virtues of the ideal type of employee-centered supervisor. And, fortunately, no one supervisor has all the bad traits found in many production-centered supervisors. We should remember that the various practices that researchers have fond which distinguish these two kinds of supervision represent the many practices and methods of supervisors of all gradations between these extremes. We should be careful, too, of the implications of the labels attached to the two types. For instance, being production-centered is not necessarily bad, since the principal responsibility of any supervisor is maintaining the production level that is expected of his work group. Being employee-centered may not necessarily be good, if the only result is a happy, chuckling crew of loafers. To return to the researchers' findings, employee-centered supervisors:

- Recommend promotions, transfers, pay increases
- Inform men about what is happening in the company
- Keep men posted on how well they are doing
- Hear complaints and grievances sympathetically
- Speak up for subordinates

Production-centered supervisors, on the other hand, don't do those things. They check on employees more frequently, give more detailed and frequent instructions, don't give reasons for changes, and are more punitive when mistakes are made. Employee-centered supervisors were reported to contribute to high morale and high production, whereas production-centered supervision was associated with lower morale and less production.

More recent findings, however, show that the relationship between supervision and productivity is not this simple. Investigators now report that high production is more frequently associated with supervisory practices which combine employee-centered behavior with concern for production. (This concern is not the same, however, as anxiety about production, which is the hallmark of our production-centered supervisor.) Let us examine these apparently contradictory findings and the premises from which they are derived.

SUPERVISION AND MORALE

Why do supervisory activities cause high or low production? As the name implies, the activities of the employee-centered supervisor tend to relate him more closely and satisfactorily to his workers. The production-centered supervisor's practices tend to separate him from his group and to foster antagonism. An analysis of this difference may answer our question.

Earlier, we pointed out that the supervisor is a type of leader and that leadership is intimately related to the group in which it occurs We discover, now, that an employee-centered supervisor's primary activities are concerned with both his leadership and his group membership. Such a supervisor is a member of a group and occupies a leadership role in that group.

These facts are sometimes obscured when we speak of the supervisor as management's representative, or as the organizational link between management and the employee, or as the end of the chain of command. If we really want to understand what it is we expect of the supervisor, we must remember that he is the designated leader of a group of employees to whom he is bound by interaction and interdependence.

Most of his actions are aimed, consciously or unconsciously, at strengthening membership ties in the group. This includes both making members more conscious that he is a member of their group) and causing members to identify themselves more closely with the group. These ends are accomplished by:

- making the group more attractive to the worker: they find satisfaction of their needs for recognition, friendship, enjoyable work, etc.;
- maintaining open communication: employees can express their views and obtain information about the organization
- giving assistance: members can seek advice on personal problems as well as their work; and
- acting as a buffer between the group and management: he speaks up for his men and explains the reasons for management's decisions.

Such actions both strengthen group cohesiveness and solidarity and affirm the supervisor's leadership position in the group.

DEFINING MORALE

This brings us back to a point mentioned earlier. We had said that employee-centered supervisors contribute to high morale as well as to high production. But how can we explain units which have low morale and high productivity, or vice versa? Usually production and morale are considered separately, partly because they are measured against different criteria and partly because, in some instances, they seem to be independent of each other.

Some of this difficulty may stem from confusion over definitions of morale. Morale has been defined as, or measured by, absences from work, satisfaction with job or company, dissension among members of work groups, productivity, apathy or lack of interest, readiness to help others, and a general aura of happiness as rated by observers. Some of these criteria of morale are not subject to the influence of the supervisor, and some of them are not clearly related to productivity. Definitions like these invite findings of low morale coupled with high production.

Both productivity and morale can be influenced by environmental factors not under the control of group members or supervisors. Such things as plant layout, organizational structure and goals, lighting, ventilation, communications, and management planning may have an adverse or desirable effect.

We might resolve the dilemma by defining morale on the basis of our understanding of the supervisor as leader of a group; morale is the degree of satisfaction of group members with their leadership. In this light, the supervisor's employee-centered activities bear a clear relation to morale. His efforts to increase employee identification with the group and to strengthen his leadership lead to greater satisfaction with that leadership. By increasing group cohesiveness and by demonstrating that his influence and power can aid the group, he is able to enhance his leadership status and afford satisfaction to the group.

SUPERVISION, PRODUCTION, AND MORALE

There are factors within the organization itself which determine whether increased production is possible:

- Are production goals expressed in terms understandable to employees and are they realistic?
- Do supervisors responsible for production respect the agency mission and production goals?
- If employees do not know how to do the job well, does management provide a trainer—often the supervisor—who can teach efficient work methods?

There are other factors within the work group which determine whether increased production will be attained:

- Is leadership present which can bring about the desired level of production?
- Are production goals accepted by employees as reasonable and attainable?
- If group effort is involved, are members able to coordinate their efforts?

Research findings confirm the view that an employee-centered supervisor can achieve higher morale than a production-centered supervisor. Managers may well ask what is the relationship between this and production.

Supervision is production-oriented to the extent that it focuses attention on achieving organizational goals, and plans and devises methods for attaining them; it is employee-centered to the extent that it focuses attention on employee attitudes toward those goals, and plans and works toward maintenance of employee satisfaction.

High productivity and low morale result when a supervisor plans and organizes work efficiently but cannot achieve high membership satisfaction. Low production and high morale result when a supervisor, though keeping members satisfied with his leadership, either has not gained acceptance of organizational goals or does not have the technical competence to achieve them.

The relationship between supervision, morale, and productivity is an interdependent one, with the supervisor playing an integral role due to his ability to influence productivity and morale independently of each other.

A supervisor who can plan his work well has good technical knowledge, and who can install better production methods can raise production without necessarily increasing group satisfaction. On the other hand, a supervisor who can motivate his employees and keep them satisfied with his leadership can gain high production in spite of technical difficulties and environmental obstacles.

CLIMATE AND SUPERVISION

Climate, the intangible environment of an organization made up of attitudes, beliefs, and traditions, plays a large part in morale, productivity, and supervision. Usually when we speak of climate and its relationship to morale and productivity, we talk about the merits of *democratic* versus *authoritarian* climate. Employees seem to produce more and have higher morale in a democratic climate, whereas in an authoritarian climate, the reverse seems to be true or so the researchers tell us. We would do well to determine what these terms mean to supervision.

Perhaps most of our difficulty in understanding and applying these concepts comes from our emotional reactions to the words themselves. For example, authoritarian climate is usually painted as the very blackest kind of dictatorship. This is not surprising, because we are usually expected to believe that it is invariably bad. Conversely, democratic climate is drawn to make the driven snow look impure by comparison.

Now these descriptions are most probably true when we talk about our political processes, or town meetings, or freedom of speech. However, the same labels have been used by social scientists in other contexts and have also been applied to government and business organizations, without it, it seems, any recognition that the meanings and their social values may have changed somewhat

For example, these labels were used in experiments conducted in an informal classroom setting using 11-year-old boys as subjects. The descriptive labels applied to the climate of the setting as well as the type of leadership practiced. When these labels were transferred to a management setting, it seems that many presumed that they principally meant the king of leadership rather than climate. We can see that there is a great difference between the experimental and management settings and that leadership practices for one might be inappropriate for the other.

It is doubtful that formal work organizations can be anything but authoritarian, in that goals are set by management and a hierarchy exists through which decisions and orders from the top are transmitted downward. Organizations are authoritarian by structure and need; direction and control are placed in the hands of a few in order to gain fast and efficient decision making. Now this does not mean to describe a dictatorship. It is merely the recognition of the fact that direction of organizational affairs comes from above. It should be noted that leadership in some natural groups is, in this sense, authoritarian.

Granting that formal organizations have this kind of authoritarian leadership, can there be a democratic climate? Certainly there can be, but we would want to define and delimit this term. A more realistic meaning of democratic climate in organizations is the use of permissive and participatory methods in management-employee relations. That is, a mutual exchange of information and explanation with the granting of individual freedom within certain restricted and defined limits. However, it is not our purpose to debate the merits of authoritarianism versus democracy. We recognize that within the small work group there is a need for freedom from constraint and an increase in participation in order to achieve organizational goals within the framework of the organizational movement.

Another aspect of climate is best expressed by this familiar, and true, saying: actions speak louder than words. Of particular concern to us is this effect of management climate on the behavior of supervisors, particularly in employee-centered activities.

There have been reports of disappointment with efforts to make supervisors ore employee-centered. Managers state that, since research has shown ways of improving human relations, supervisors should begin to practice these methods. Usually a training course in human relations is established; and supervisors are given this training. Managers then sit back and wait for the expected improvements, only to find that there are none.

If we wish to produce changes in the supervisor's behavior, the climate must be made appropriate and rewarding to the changed behavior. This means that top-level attitudes and behavior cannot deny or contradict the change we are attempting to effect. Basic changes in organizational behavior cannot be made with any permanence, unless we provide an environment that is receptive to the changes and rewards those persons who do change.

IMPROVING SUPERVISION

Anyone who has read this far might expect to find *A Dozen Rules for Dealing With Employees* or *29 Steps to Supervisory Success*. We will not provide such a list.

Simple rules suffer from their simplicity. They ignore the complexities of human behavior. Reliance upon rules may cause supervisors to concentrate on superficial aspects of their relations with employees. It may preclude genuine understanding.

The supervisor who relies on a list of rules tends to think of people in mechanistic terms. In a certain situation, he uses *Rule No. 3*. Employees are not treated as thinking and feeling persons, but rather as figures in a formula: Rule 3 applied to employee X = Production.

Employees usually recognize mechanical manipulation and become dissatisfied and resentful. They lose faith in, and respect for, their supervisor, and this may be reflected in lower morale and productivity.

We do not mean that supervisors must become social science experts if they wish to improve. Reports of current research indicate that there are two major parts of their job which can be strengthened through self-improvement: (1) Work planning, including technical skills, and (2) motivation of employees.

The most effective supervisors combine excellence in the administrative and technical aspects of their work with friendly and considerate personal relations with their employees.

CRITICAL PERSONAL RELATIONS

Later in this chapter we shall talk about administrative aspects of supervision, but first let us comment on *friendly and considerate personal relations*. We have discussed this subject throughout the preceding chapters, but we want to review some of the critical supervisory influences on personal relations.

Closeness of Supervision: The closeness of supervision has an important effect on productivity and morale. Mann and Dent found that supervisors of low-producing units supervise very closely, while high-producing supervisors exercise only general supervision. It was found that the low-producing supervisors:

- check on employees more frequently
- give more detailed and frequent instructions
- limit employee's freedom to do job in own way

Workers who felt less closely supervised reported that they were better satisfied with their jobs and the company. We should note that the manner or attitude of the supervisor has an important bearing on whether employees perceive supervision as being close or general.

These findings are another way of saying that supervision does not mean standing over the employee and telling him what to do and when and how to do it. The more effective supervisor tells his employees what is required, giving general instructions.

COMMUNICATION

Supervisors of high-production units consider communication as one of the most important aspects of their job. Effective communication is used by these supervisors to achieve better interpersonal relations and improved employee motivation. Low-production supervisors do not rate communications as highly important.

High-producing supervisors find that an important aid to more effective communication is listening. They are ready to listen to both personal problems or interests and questions about the work. This does not mean that they are *nosey* or meddle in their employees' personal lives, but rather that they show a willingness to listen, and do listen, if their employees wish to discuss problems.

These supervisors inform employees about forthcoming changes in work; they discuss agency policy with employees; and they make sure that each employee knows how well he is doing. What these supervisors do is use two-way communication effectively. Unless the supervisor freely imparts information, he will not receive information in return.

Attitudes and perception are frequently affected by communication or the lack of it. Research surveys reveal that many supervisors are not aware of their employees' attitudes, nor do they know what personal reactions their supervision arouses. Through frank discussion with employees, they have been surprised to discover employee beliefs about which they were ignorant. Discussion sometimes reveals that the supervisor and his employees have totally different impressions about the same event. The supervisor should be constantly on the alert for misconceptions about his words and deeds. He must remember that, although his actions are perfectly clear to himself, they may be, and frequently are, viewed differently by employees.

Failure to communicate information results in misconceptions and false assumptions. What you say and how you say it will strongly affect your employees' attitudes and perceptions. By giving them available information, you can prevent misconceptions; by discussion, you may be able to change attitudes; by questioning, you can discover what the perceptions and assumptions really are. And it need hardly be added that actions should conform very closely to words.

If we were to attempt to reduce the above discussion on communication to rules, we would have a long list which would be based on one cardinal principle: Don't make assumptions!

- Don't assume that your employees know; tell them.
- Don't assume that you know how they feel; find out.
- Don't assume that they understand; clarify.

20 SUPERVISORY HINTS

1. Avoid inconsistency.
2. Always give employees a chance to explain their action before taking disciplinary action. Don't allow too much time for a "cooling off" period before disciplining an employee.
3. Be specific in your criticisms.
4. Delegate responsibility wisely.
5. Do not argue or lose your temper, and avoid being impatient.
6. Promote mutual respect and be fair, impartial, and open-minded.
7. Keep in mind that asking for employees' advice and input can be helpful in decision making.
8. If you make promises, keep them.
9. Always keep the feelings, abilities, dignity and motives of your staff in mind.
10. Remain loyal to your employees' interests.
11. Never criticize employees in front of others, or treat employees like children.
12. Admit mistakes. Don't place blame on your employees, or make excuses.
13. Be reasonable in your expectations, give complete instructions, and establish well-planned goals.
14. Be knowledgeable about office details and procedures, but avoid becoming bogged down in details.
15. Avoid supervising too closely or too loosely. Employees should also view you as an approachable supervisor.
16. Remember that employees' personal problems may affect job performance, but become involved only when appropriate.
17. Work to develop workers, and to instill a feeling of cooperation while working toward mutual goals.
18. Do not overpraise or underpraise, be properly appreciative.
19. Never ask an employee to discipline someone for you.
20. A complaint, even if unjustified, should be taken seriously.

NOTES

www.ingramcontent.com/pod-product-compliance
Lightning Source LLC
Chambersburg PA
CBHW081829300426
44116CB00014B/2526